Joanna Kosloff

Newfoundlands

Everything about Purchase, Care, Nutrition,
Breeding, Behavior, and Training

With 46 Color Photographs

Illustrations by Tana Hakanson

BARRON'S

Dedication
This book is dedicated to my most beloved boy: La Foi's Dylan Malloy de Tomas.

© Copyright 1996 by Barron's Educational Series, Inc.

All inquiries should be addressed to:
Barron's Educational Series, Inc.
250 Wireless Boulevard
Hauppauge, NY 11788

International Standard Book No. 0-8120-9489-1

Library of Congress Catalog Card No. 95-41068

Library of Congress Cataloging-in-Publication Data
Kosloff, Joanna.
   Newfoundlands : everything about purchase, care, nutrition, diseases, breeding, behavior, and training / Joanna Kosloff ; drawings by Tana Hakanson.
      p.   cm. — (A complete pet owner's manual)
   Includes bibliographical references (p. 96) and index.
      ISBN 0-8120-9489-1
      1. Newfoundland dog. I. Title. II. Series.
   SF429.N4K67   1996   95-41068
   636.7'3—dc20   CIP

Printed in Hong Kong

6789   9955   9876543

About the Author
Joanna Kosloff is the editor-in-chief of a national entertainment magazine. She is also a novelist and television writer and has owned and loved Irish setters for twenty-five years. She currently shows her three setters in conformation and obedience. She recently finished her Irish setter dog, CH Fleetwood Farm's Jamie O'Dyl, a great great grandson of the most winning Irish setter in the history of the breed, Fleetwood Farm's CH Starheir's Aaron Ardee. Ms. Kosloff is a member of the Irish Setter Club of America and active in rescue efforts. She is presently working on several other dog breed books.

Photo Credits
Judi Adler: back cover, pages 17, 24, 46 bottom right, 49; Barbara Augello: front cover, page 20 top and bottom; Donna J. Coss: pages 9 top, 16; Chet Jezierski: pages 42 bottom, 43 top left and bottom left, 56, 65 top, 77, 81; Larry Johnson: page 8; Bob Schwartz: inside front cover, inside back cover, pages 4, 5, 9 bottom, 12, 13 top and bottom, 21, 29, 32, 38 top left, top right, and bottom, 39, 43 top right, 46 top, 61, 65 bottom, 68, 72, 84, 85, 89, 92, 93; Judith Strom: pages 42 top, 46 bottom, 53, 60, 64, 69.

Important Note
This pet owner's guide tells the reader how to buy and care for a Newfoundland dog. The author and the publisher consider it important to point out that the advice given in the book is meant primarily for normally developed puppies from a good breeder—that is, dogs of excellent physical health and good character.

Anyone who adopts a fully grown dog should be aware that the animal has already formed its basic impressions of human beings. The new owner should watch the animal carefully, including its behavior toward humans, and should meet the previous owner. If the dog comes from a shelter, it may be possible to get some information on the dog's background and peculiarities there. There are dogs that, as a result of bad experiences with humans, behave in an unnatural manner or may even bite. Only people that have experience with dogs should take in such animals.

Caution is further advised in the association of children with dogs, in meeting with other dogs, and in exercising the dog without a leash.

Even well-behaved and carefully supervised dogs sometimes do damage to someone else's property or cause accidents. It is therefore in the owner's interest to be adequately insured against such eventualities, and we strongly urge all dog owners to purchase a liability policy that covers their dog.

Contents

Over the centuries, the Newfoundland has been known as a helpmate as well as a devoted and loyal companion to his human master.

Preface

Man's Best Friend— the Newfoundland

Perhaps more than any other breed, the Newfoundland's very existence depended upon its ability to interact in a meaningful and productive manner with its human masters. Farmers, fishermen, and tradesmen depended on the Newf as a working partner, while families counted on it to literally carry its load of responsibilities. This close proximity to humans would not have been possible if the Newf had not been a willing and eager participant endowed with a sweet, gentle disposition and an innate intelligence. More than most breeds, it has a need to bond with people and to give and receive affection. The Newf is also very protective of its human family and will go to any lengths to insure their safety. Though not a barker, it will alert its family to any situation that deviates from normal. Despite its large size, it is extremely gentle and for that reason makes a wonderful companion for children. In 1989 a young Newfy bitch, Dirigo's Magnificent Villa, CD (Companion Dog), received a special presidential award for heroism after jumping the six-foot fence in her kennel to respond to the cries of a child trapped under a snowdrift. The courageous Newf tracked after the little girl in the blinding storm and trampled the snow, pulling her out and carrying her home to safety. Feats such as this are commonplace among this breed whose primary concern is the safety and well-being of its human family.

Acknowledgments

To those fanciers of the breed who have so generously shared their time, their stories, and their precious Newfs with me, I am exceedingly grateful. Thanks to Grace Freedson for getting me started on this exciting journey. Special thanks to Newf owner, Dawn Hockman, who is very active in the rescue effort, for introducing me to the breed. During all the hours she spoke to me, her Newfs were gathered at our feet listening, perhaps even ruefully adding their own silent commentary. I would also like to thank Judi Adler of Sweetbay Newfoundlands for her beautiful books and photographs as well as for her time and encouragement. Most especially, deep appreciation goes to my editor, Mary Falcon, whose knowledge, patience, and humor guided me over some long, winding roads. And many thanks to Joe Stahlkuppe, a fellow fancier and writer, whose suggestions led me to write this book. Thank you to Dr. Theodore Leif and the staff of Acacia Animal Clinic in Pompano Beach, Florida, for their answers to many technical questions. Thanks to Dr. Dan Rice for his suggestions. Finally, I would like to thank my husband, George, and my most beloved red boys: Ch Fleetwood Farm's Jamie O' Dyl and Fleetwood's Right About You—Dylan and Brandy. And to Sweet Baby James—Jamie— our Irish rescue boy who has insinuated his way into our lives and our hearts and who patiently waited at the door with a ball in his mouth until I finished the last chapter of this book!

Joanna Kosloff

Understanding Newfoundlands

The Newfoundland as we know it today has come to us through time as a mixture of fact and fancy, a mingling of history and legend. That is due, in part at least, to the great love and high esteem in which man has held this great black dog over the centuries. The human owner's need to brag and boast about the achievements and wondrous deeds of this canine companion may have slightly embellished many a tale about the exploits of this extraordinary breed. Even so, it only serves to underscore how beloved the Newfoundland really is. It has been said that nowhere else in the canine world can one find a breed more loyal, trustworthy, gentle, and innately intelligent than the Newfoundland. Over the centuries this giant dog has been a

When some proud son of man returns to earth,
Unknown to glory, but upheld by birth,
The sculptor's art exhausts the pomp of woe,
And storied urns record who rests below;
When all is done, upon the tomb is seen,
Not what he was, but what he should have been.
But the poor dog, in life the firmest friend,
The first to welcome, foremost to defend,
Whose honest heart is still his master's won,
Who labours, fights, lives, breathes for him alone,
Unhonour'd falls, unnoticed all his worth,
Denied in heaven the soul he held on earth:
While man, vain insect! hopes to be forgiven
And claims himself a sole exclusive heaven.
Oh man! thou feeble tenant of an hour,
Debased by slavery, or corrupt by power,
Who knows thee well must quit thee with disgust,
Degraded mass of animated dust!
Thy love is lust, thy friendship all a cheat,
Thy smiles hypocrisy, thy words deceit!
By nature vile, ennobled but by name,
Each kindred brute might bid thee blush for shame.
Ye! who perchance behold this simple urn,
Pass on — it honours none you wish to mourn.
To mark a friend's remains these stones arise;
I never knew but one — and there he lies.
— Lord Byron

Epitaph to a Dog

Near this spot are deposited the remains of one who possessed beauty without vanity, strength without insolence, courage without ferocity, and all the virtues of man without his vices. This praise, which would be unmeaning flattery if inscribed over human ashes, is but a just tribute to the memory of Boatswain, a dog who was born at Newfoundland May, 1803 and died at Newstead Abbey Nov. 18, 1808

devoted helpmate, constant companion, and savior in times of trouble. While many canines have been singled out in literature, perhaps none has been better immortalized than the Newfoundland as evidenced by the poem written by the nineteenth-century English romantic poet, George Gordon, Lord Byron, upon the death of his beloved Newf, Boatswain.

Byron acquired the big black Newfoundland when he was a young boy living at his ancestral home, Newstead Abbey. Boatswain was the poet's constant companion and bosom friend. In fact, when the Newf died, Byron vowed to be buried in the same grave when he met his own

Though initially thought to be a different breed, the black and white Landseer must be bred back to the black Newfoundland every few generations to maintain type.

end. Unfortunately, it didn't work out that way, as Lord Byron died while fighting in a civil war in Greece. But even at the end he had another Newf named Lyon by his side. The poet's own words about the dog sum up the depth of his sentiment: "Thou are more faithful than men, Lyon. I trust thee more." What a compliment! After Byron breathed his last, Lyon was shipped back to England where he lived out his days with a close friend of the poet.

Origins and History of the Breed

The ancient people dubbed the Newfoundland "the hero dog" because of its renowned and selfless feats of bravery. Poets extolled it for its loyal and loving nature, while artists immortalized it as a gentle giant whose bond with its human companions was irrevocable. It is one of the only breeds that has ever been honored by having its picture on a postage stamp.

The Newfoundland is a large, strong, heavy-coated dog whose versatility on land and in water is unparalleled; a faithful companion who has found its way into more legends than even the most conscientious historian can recount; an imposing figure that impresses the eye with its great dignity and pride. In motion, the Newfoundland gives the impression of effortless power. It is both literally and figuratively, a dog for all seasons.

There's an old saying that goes something like this: "Show me your companions and I'll tell you what you are." This truism has probably never been quite so applicable as it is in the case of the breed we now know as the Newfoundland. Indeed the "Newf," or "Newfy," as it is affectionately called, has had at least a passing acquaintance with more canine species in its evolution than practically any other breed in existence today. Various reports trace its origins to no less than three different continents: Asia, Europe, and North America. Ask any fancier of the breed and you're bound to be flooded with a flurry of tales, part whimsical, part factual, about how this great dog found its way into the history books. One of the earliest and more colorful legends has it that the original ancestor of this loyal and stately breed first appeared on the North American continent about A.D. 1000 aboard an ancient Viking ship. This formidable black "bear dog" named Oolam supposedly served as a trusty mate beside its master, Norse explorer, Leif Erikson.

Still another narrative puts a Newf at the front lines of a campaign led by Napoleon I, where the dog is said to have rescued the "little general" from drowning. Even Napoleon's arch enemy, Admiral Lord Nelson, kept a Newf beside him in battle. Another account relates the daring deeds of

Due to its massive size and adaptability, the Newfoundland can effortlessly perform a variety of tasks.

The Newf's natural swimming ability, combined with its webbed feet and durable double coat, make it the perfect water dog.

one QueQue, an American Newf owned by the colonist, Samuel Adams. The story goes that while the redcoats blockaded Boston Harbor, this great black dog did its patriotic best by being such an unrelenting pest and prankster that the British soldiers were only too happy to accept defeat and return home. In 1802 another American Newfoundland named Scannon gained its place in history by accompanying the explorers Lewis and Clark on their Northwest expedition. According to reports, Scannon was kidnapped by a group of Indians who apparently had him earmarked for a tribal banquet. But Lewis and Clark were so incensed about losing their valuable teammate that they sent out a search-and-rescue party to bring the dog back. When faced with such a formidable show of force, Scannon's captors put their dinner plans on hold and handed the great dog over.

An Ancient Breed

Though there are no early written records of the breed, it is generally accepted that the Newfoundland is one of the oldest species of dogs in existence. It is probably a combination of several different canines, including the Great Pyrenees, Basque spaniels, different varieties of sheepdogs, the Tibetan Mastiff, and the Norse bear dog. However, even before the Viking explorers landed on the North American continent, skeletal remains of giant dogs dating back to the fifth century A.D. were found in Indian gravesites. They had triangular-shaped heads, pointy, somewhat elongated muzzles, erect ears, and curled tails.

By the sixteenth century, French, English, Basque, Spanish, and Portuguese fishermen established settlements in Newfoundland, and it's reasonable to assume they brought their dogs with them and that these dogs bred with the native population.

This may account for the two different color strains that developed in the breed: the self-colored Newfoundland, which is an all-black, brown, or gray dog, occasionally with a white blaze, and the Landseer, a predominately white dog with black markings. Today, the two are simply considered color variations of the same breed.

The Breed Today

The breed as we know it probably originated in the easternmost Canadian province of Newfoundland, from which it derives its name. From an etching, we know that the dogs of this period had elongated muzzles, triangular heads, and sparse furnishings. It wasn't until 1775 that the breed was officially named by George Cartwright, a native Newfoundlander who ascribed the name of his island to his pet dog. Ironically, five years later the Newf was in serious danger of extinction after a government proclamation limited the ownership of the giant dogs to one per household. All others were slated to be destroyed or exported. Because of its great size and strength, however, the Newf already occupied an intrinsic place in the daily flow of commerce, so most people ignored the ordinance. It's fairly easy to understand why. The Newf pulled heavy loads, helped to haul in fishing nets and wood from the forest, powered the blacksmith's bellows, and was even known to serve as a nanny for children! When hitched to a cart, it was able to navigate its load through narrow streets a horse and buggy could not. In short, the Newf was such a fine laborer and worked so well at the side of its human charges that it was far too valuable to do without.

The dog we now recognize as the Newfoundland was largely developed in both England and America in the nineteenth century. The first recorded showing of the Newfoundland was at a dog show in Birmingham, England, in 1860. Soon after, an all-black Newf named Nero, owned by the Prince of Wales, became the first Newfoundland to gain prominence in the show ring. By the late eighteenth century the Newf had made its way south from Canada to the United States. The first American champion was Sam in 1883. Thirty years later Major II won his championship. In 1908 Graydon's New Jersey Big Boy, a Landseer who was imported from England, became the third Newf to attain an American championship. Though the breed became very popular in the United States, it wasn't granted official AKC (American Kennel Club) status until 1914.

Besides the eighteenth-century proclamation, the breed had two other major setbacks in its development. During World War I, because of food rationing and the amount of food they required, Newfs nearly disappeared from England; the same occurred during World War II. But due to the dedication of a few breeders, the stock, though depleted, remained strong and of high quality. In fact, in the 1920s American and Canadian breeders began importing English stock to fortify their own. In this endeavor, one dog stands out above the rest: English Champion Siki, also known as the "father of champions." Above all others, the Siki line laid the foundation for most of the successful breeding programs in the United States and Canada. Though not a spectacular specimen of the breed, Ch. Siki was nonetheless one of the most prepotent sires in the history of the breed, producing progeny of extraordinary quality. Most kennels operating today can trace their lines back to this all-important Siki bloodline. Thanks to the efforts of a small number of dedicated breeders, this great dog thrives and prospers in breeding programs today.

Black versus Landseer

Although it is now accepted among fanciers of the breed that the black Newfoundland and the Landseer are one and the same breed, some historians have pointed out that the two were initially separated geographically and may have a combination of different breeds in their ancestry. The Landseer was named after the English artist, Sir Edwin Landseer, who painted many black-and-white Newfoundlands. In fact, the first English Newfoundland champion was a Landseer called Dick, who had a black head with a white blaze and saddle, black rump, and a white tail. It is also interesting to note that the black-and-white Landseer must be bred back to black Newfoundland stock at a fairly regular interval in order to maintain type. Otherwise, the Landseer becomes more refined looking with an elongated muzzle and narrower body and head, like its early ancestors.

Characteristics of the Breed

When one comes face to face with a full-grown Newfoundland for the first time, it is an experience one is not likely to forget. The Newf's formidable proportions, its awesome musculature, and dignified bearing give the most casual observer some moments for pause and unwitting admiration. But even those who may be initially intimidated by its great size are soon won over by the amazing gentleness and sweet disposition of this fine dog. As in any breed, some Newfs have better dispositions than others, but it is very rare to come across a Newfoundland with a nasty or mean temperament. When this does occur, it is almost always a consequence of poor breeding that results when dogs are indiscriminately bred, without regard to preserving good characteristics and eliminating bad ones. It may also be attributed to abuse.

Besides the self-colored all-black dog, Newfoundlands can also be brown, gray, or predominately white with black markings (Landseer) in color.

While the Newf can be classified as a *giant* breed, it is not an overly active dog, so its exercise requirements are not rigorous. It loves to play and is equally at home on land or in water. Its unique swimming ability and webbed feet make it the penultimate water dog. The Newfoundland is also one of the most versatile breeds. Its double, water-resistant coat insulates it from extremes in temperatures, making it easily adaptable to either hot or cold weather. More than anything else, the most striking characteristic of the Newf is its desire to be with humans. The Newfoundland is definitely a "people" dog.

We've all heard the expression, "You can dress it up but you can't take it out." Nothing could be further from the truth when talking about the Newfoundland. Whether at a family picnic or dinner at the White House, the properly trained Newf always minds its manners. It may plop its head in your lap on occasion for a friendly pat, but it's not likely to jump up and make a nuisance of itself. As long as it is with its family, the Newf is content to curl up in a favorite spot until you instruct it otherwise.

The Newf is also a natural-born protector. It is especially drawn to children. In fact, there are many stories of affluent families in the nineteenth century employing the Newfoundland as a nanny for their children. A gregarious dog, the Newfy will generally walk up and freely greet people, but if it is uncertain, it will stand at attention and evaluate the situation. Many Newf owners swear their dogs have a sixth sense when it comes to sizing up potential trouble. Just imagine the imposing sight of this massive dog standing at attention. It's enough to make even the most brazen potential perpetrator think twice!

Disadvantages of the Breed

Even though the Newfoundland is an extremely gentle and affable breed, its size does pose some disadvantages. For example, one of its least attractive characteristics is drooling. Because dogs sweat not through their skin but through their mouths, panting is nature's only way of cooling them down. Since Newfs have such large mouths, they do have a tendency to drool profusely, particularly when hot or excited, and some people may find this objectionable. The Newf can also be a bit of a slobberer when drinking water. Indeed, this "water baby" may find it amusing to submerge its whole muzzle in the water bowl and then shake off the excess water unceremoniously all over the kitchen floor. But the true Newf fancier finds these characteristics more engaging than annoying.

The Newfoundland is an all-around outdoor dog, but its webbed feet and double water-resistant coat makes it particularly adapted to swimming.

13

Be forewarned, Newfies are not for everyone. Many an impulse buyer will fall in love with a teddy bear-like puppy only to become horrified several months down the line when Junior begins to tip the scale at over 100 pounds (45 kg). But for the prospective owner who wants a large, multipurpose dog possessed of great intelligence, true loyalty, and an even temperament, a well-bred Newfoundland is a joy that owner will treasure forever.

The Newf is also an attention seeker and a bit of a ham. In its quest to be noticed, it can be a downright pest at times! Many a Newfoundland owner will tell amusing stories about how their Newfs compete for affection. This loyal and loving dog is happiest when sitting at the foot of its owner receiving an affectionate pat on the head. Even though the Newfoundland loves people, it is not a "one-man dog." But it *will* tend to play favorites within a family, and spend the most time with the person who gives it the most attention.

As with any other breed, to insure that the Newfoundland reaches its full potential as a companion dog, early training is essential and, since the Newf is a working breed, it is particularly adaptable to instruction and takes pride in a task well done.

Considerations Before You Buy

Owning a Giant Breed Dog

There are few things more appealing than a litter of cuddly Newfoundland puppies. They are sure to tickle your funny bone and warm your heart. But wait! Before you get ready to scoop one up and take it home, be sure you know what you're getting into. An eight-week-old pup may be a joy to behold, but take a look at its parents before you make a final decision. Are you physically and psychologically ready to assume the care of a giant breed dog? That cute little 15-pound (6.8 kg) pup will be tipping the scales at about 130 pounds (59 kg) by the time it's a year old. Can you handle that? Even though you've probably read several books about the breed, and have decided the Newf is the dog for you, it's one thing to be intellectually aware of what's involved with owning a Newf, but it's quite another thing to see a full-grown adult in the flesh. If you're not intimidated, then you've definitely settled on one of the most loyal and loving breeds out there.

Be aware, however, that loving the breed is not a good enough reason to own a Newfoundland. Your lifestyle will have to accommodate its needs as it grows and matures. If you live in an apartment, the Newf is probably not the right dog for you. Since Newfs love the outdoors, you should have a reasonably large, fenced-in yard in which the dog can romp. Are you able to spend the time and money required to care for a giant breed like the Newf? Remember, it will have daily grooming requirements. It will also have to be trained while it is a puppy so that, when it reaches adulthood, you won't have an unruly giant dog on your hands. Do you have the time to do this? Will other members of the family be responsible for your Newf's care? If so, be certain they know what role they will play in its growth and development.

Under no circumstances should you buy a Newf for a child and then make the child responsible for the dog's care. We've all heard a parent tell a child, "You can have the dog as long as you take care of it." This is absolutely the wrong reason to buy a Newf or any dog, for that matter. Not only is this attitude terribly unfair to the dog, but it also sets a bad example for the child who will come to believe that all living things are disposable. Unless you are prepared to make your Newf a member of the family and be responsible for it for the rest of its life, resist the impulse to buy—get a stuffed animal instead. If more people gave serious thought to dog ownership and its responsibilities, there would be far fewer dogs euthanized in shelters across the country each year. Think about that before you purchase your Newf or any other pet.

Above all, you must be honest with yourself. The world is filled with dog fanciers. Some prefer to admire their canine friends from afar. Others prefer to share their lives with a pet. One is not better than the other. Just know what type of a fancier you are or you will be unfair to yourself and the pet

Despite its great size, the Newfoundland is an extremely gentle dog and bonds closely with humans, particularly children.

you bring into your home. A person with a very busy lifestyle or heavy career or family demands probably will not have the time to care for a Newf, despite all the good intentions in the world. That's why it's important to be realistic and honest before anticipating the purchase of a Newfoundland.

Where to Start

If you've met every possible objection to owning a Newf and you still want to go full steam ahead, then you're ready to get serious. Where do you go next? A good start would be local dog shows. There, you cannot only see many different types of the breed, but also meet many Newfoundland breeders and learn about their breeding programs and bloodlines, as well as the availability of dogs/puppies. Once you've taken a

few names and addresses, visit the breeders who impressed you the most. You'll be able to judge a well-kept kennel from a poorly maintained one fairly quickly. A kennel doesn't have to be elaborate, but it should be spotless. All resident dogs should look well cared for and well groomed. Kennels should be free of odors and be roomy enough for a giant dog like the Newf to be comfortable.

If you are unable to visit Newfoundland breeders, you can buy your dog sight unseen and still be very comfortable with your choice. The Newfoundland Club of America publishes a breeders' directory that you can use to contact different breeders. If one breeder doesn't have dogs available, he or she will usually recommend another breeder. By talking to several breeders, you will soon

Before buying a Newfoundland, be aware that a cute, cuddly puppy will soon grow into a 120- to 130-pound adult dog.

get a feeling for what you want in your dog. Good breeders are proud of their reputations and are happy to supply the prospective buyer with references. Once you think you've found the right kennel, the breeder will send you a pedigree upon request. When you receive it, compare the bloodlines to those in a breed book you have purchased beforehand and you'll learn a lot a more about your prospective pup. If it's a match, congratulations! You've just selected a companion who will be your most trusted friend for as long as it lives. If you live too far away from your breeder to go and pick up your Newf, the breeder will arrange to ship it to you on a commercial airline.

Pet Stores

Although Newfoundlands do not usually turn up in local pet stores,

occasionally one does appear. Before you decide to buy from a pet store, be sure the establishment is reputable. Ask to see the dog's pedigree and make certain it does not come from a "puppy mill." Puppy mill pups, from establishments that do large-volume, indiscriminate breeding, should be avoided. Unfortunately, these are the pups that usually end up in retail pet stores. On the other hand, some pet stores deal with local breeders and are proud of the lines they carry. If that's the case, the establishment will be happy to provide you with the documentation you require before you decide to purchase a pet.

Newspaper Ads

Another source is the newspaper. In the classified section, you'll see an area designated for pet ads. Often, small, local breeders use newspaper ads as a means of advertising and selling their litters. When calling about a puppy ad, be very straightforward in your questions. Ask what the breeding lines are, if the parents are on the premises, and if health records are available. If you're happy with the responses you get, ask to see the puppies.

Puppy versus Older Dog

Once you have made up your mind that the Newfoundland is the right breed for you, the next thing you'll want to consider is whether to get a puppy or an older dog. There are pros and cons to each, but ultimately, your decision may depend on your lifestyle.

Puppies are cute and cuddly but they are also a lot of work. If you decide on a pup, you will need to spend much more time with it than you would with an older dog that is already housebroken and probably trained. Here's where your lifestyle comes into play. In a two-career household, where Mom and Dad go out to work every day and the kids go to school, a puppy may not fit into that busy equation. However, a well-behaved Newf that is two or three years old might be perfect. This doesn't mean that older dogs don't need time and attention, too. They do. However, they are more adaptable to your needs than a young pup would be. An adult Newf won't need to go out as often as a puppy and won't require as many play periods.

One of the problems prospective owners face if they want an older dog is their availability. Most well-bred, well-trained adult Newfs are not for sale. Occasionally, however, breeders will have adult dogs for sale to good homes. Usually, a breeder will keep several puppies from a given litter with the intention of showing them in conformation and/or obedience. Sometimes, all the dogs don't mature

into the great show specimens the breeder had hoped for. At that point, the dogs usually become available for sale as pets. This is often a good way to buy a fine older dog with excellent bloodlines.

Adult Newfs may be sold or put up for adoption through ads in the newspapers, though, unless you really get a good picture of the dog's history from the present owner, this isn't the *best* way to get an adult dog. Many times, people want to dispose of an animal because it has some kind of problem, either behavioral or physical. On the other hand, the dog could be perfectly fine, but the owners either didn't know how to deal with it or were not equipped to handle a dog with the Newf's needs. If you do buy an adult dog from someone other than from a reputable breeder, ask to see its health certificates and check with the veterinarian who has been taking care of it. Then you can go ahead with the purchase with more confidence that you've made the right choice.

Some people get into dogs because they want to show them. If that's the case, you're usually better off with a puppy that you can train yourself. Even if you have no intention of getting into the sport of dogs, you may still prefer a puppy. It is certainly one of the greatest experiences to bring a nine-week-old pup into your life and have the pleasure of raising it, bonding with it, and loving it throughout its life. If you have the time, the space, and the patience, go for it! It's an experience you'll treasure forever.

Whether you decide on a puppy or an older dog, your responsibility as an owner remains the same. Once you have taken charge of this innocent and trusting living creature, you owe it the best you can give. In return, you will be rewarded a thousandfold with uncompromising devotion, absolute love, and perfect loyalty.

Male versus Female

The decision to get a male or a female is usually a matter of personal choice or experience. Both make excellent pets. However, if you want to show your Newf, a male might be the better choice. If you purchase a show bitch (female), she cannot be spayed and you will have to contend with heat periods throughout her show career. If you are not interested in showing and simply want a loving pet, the decision might come down to which pup has the best chemistry with you, regardless of sex. Most important: Unless you plan to show and breed your pup it should be spayed or neutered!

An unneutered male can become a neighborhood nuisance. Males do tend to roam, especially if there is a female dog in heat. They also have a greater incidence of prostate cancer as they become advanced in years. Neutering, however, won't keep any male dog from going out on the town if it is not properly trained and confined to a fenced-in yard. Size may also dictate your choice. Male Newfs are larger and stronger and weigh more than females, so if that variation in size is a consideration, you might be better off with a female. As with the males, if the female is not to be shown, she should be spayed. This will not only free you from the worry of unwanted puppies, but it will be healthier for your bitch in the long run. Spayed females have less risk of mammary tumors and reproductive system diseases than non-spayed females.

To sum up, unless you have specific plans for breeding and showing your Newf, you should pick the best possible puppy you can find. You can only arrive at this decision after doing lots of homework and talking to many breeders and Newf owners. At that point, when you've narrowed down your choice to two or three dogs, the best choice will be the one that strikes your fancy the most. Male or female,

Begin teaching your Newf puppy to hold a "stack" position early on if you plan to show it in conformation.

you'll know you've chosen the best dog for you.

Pet- versus Show-Quality

One thing must be stressed from the top. "Pet"-quality is not synonymous with "inferior" quality. The difference between a "show" Newf and a "pet" Newf can be so minor that only a highly trained eye can pick it out. The official AKC standard for the breed describes the ideal Newf. Those dogs that most closely resemble the standard are considered show stock. Those that fall a little short are sold as pets. Pet Newfs are neither unattractive nor unhealthy. They simply have some feature and/or features (i.e. shorter muzzle, less chest depth, narrower skull) that makes them

If you decide to purchase a Newfoundland puppy, it will require more of your time and attention than an adult Newf.

If you plan to show your Newfoundland, one of the most important things to look for is a good head.

undesirable in the show ring. Interestingly, in any given litter of say, 12 pups, even from the very best breeder, usually no more than two or three pups will be evaluated as top show prospects. Beware of the breeder who boasts that all his or her pups are show-quality. It doesn't happen that way. A breeder is lucky to get *one* top show prospect from a litter; two or three is a rare gift.

If you are not going to show your Newf, definitely purchase a pet dog. Even if you would like to do obedience work or compete in water or tracking sports with your Newf, a pet dog is a good choice. You can still spay/neuter your Newf and compete in these areas.

If you plan to show your Newf in conformation classes (AKC-sanctioned dog shows), you will want to pick the best show specimen possible. Remember, in order to compete in conformation classes, your dog cannot be altered. The best way to decide on a show Newf is to attend all the dog shows you can prior to your selection. Even within show dogs, there is great variation. In Newfs, for example, some bloodlines carry a larger, heavier head and muzzle than others. There is also variation in color and, to a lesser degree, in size, from breeder to breeder. Some dogs move better than others. Some look better in a "stack" (standing in place in a position that best shows its conformation to the AKC standard for the breed) position. You must decide which characteristics you like best and then contact the breeders whose dogs appear to exemplify what you're looking for in your show Newf.

Be aware that, if you are purchasing a young pup, a breeder can, at best, only make an educated guess about your pup's potential as a show dog. Most reputable breeders will allow you to return the pup if it doesn't measure up to your expectation in the conformation ring. However, if you'd rather not go

Despite its great size, the Newfoundland is an extremely gentle dog and bonds closely with humans, particularly children.

through the pain of disappointment, wait and get an older pup or a young adult dog. Usually, by the time the dog is between six and eight months of age, a breeder can tell you which ones are going to be the best show prospects.

Generally, show puppies will command a higher price than pet pups. But don't go bargain hunting. Buy the best possible dog you can afford. Reputable breeders won't go into a bidding war with prospective owners. Breeders want their dogs to go to the best homes and most will be very wary of selling to someone who has come to haggle. As a prospective owner, you should also be very suspicious of the breeder who tries to push a "sale" pup on you. Often, this is a pup that the breeder has not been able to sell for

one reason or another. That doesn't mean it isn't a good dog, it just means you should be extra cautious. Sometimes a breeder will reduce the prices of a perfectly fine group of pups because they are older and he or she hasn't had any buyers. Again, this doesn't mean they're inferior dogs. By and large, there are always far more dogs of any breed available than there are buyers. Many times, you can get a very good dog at a much lower price because the pup is a little older and thus less desirable to the majority of buyers. The rule of thumb is to use common sense and exercise reasonable caution. Ask questions, talk to other breeders and Newf owners, then make an informed decision based on what you've learned.

When selecting a show Newf, choose a pup with a good head and top-line. The top-line should be fairly straight from the withers to the croup. Look for a strong front and rear, good bite, superior movement, and a sweet disposition. As it matures, you can expect to see some changes. At about 10 to 14 months, it will appear too short for its legs and its ears. Don't worry, it's just going through the "uglies" as many breeders refer to this awkward stage. In most cases, the pup will mature into a beautiful dog. (See The American Kennel Club Standard for the Newfoundland, page 60.)

Getting a Rescue Dog

Most breeds now have very active clubs that "rescue" abandoned animals. The purpose of the rescue effort in any breed is to keep track of dogs that have become homeless for one reason or another and relocate them into good, loving homes. The Newfoundland Club of America and its many regional clubs have an active breed rescue program. The rescue clubs maintain a list, by state, of Newfs available for adoption. If you don't intend to show or breed your Newf, you may want to consider getting a dog from a rescue club.

As we have discussed, people will sometimes buy a Newf without truly understanding what ownership of a giant breed entails. In such cases, the dog is either given to a local shelter, or worse, allowed to roam and become lost. In such situations, the rescue club intercedes by taking the dog, placing it in foster care, and getting it into good condition while it awaits a permanent home. Occasionally, rescue dogs are in poor condition when they're taken in because the former owners weren't willing or able to keep up with the dog's regular maintenance requirements. Sometimes, rescue dogs have temperament problems because they've

been abused. In any case, the rescue volunteer who serves as a foster home honestly assesses the dog and works with it to make it adoptable. When it's ready to go to a home, the rescue club attempts to match the personality of the dog to its new owners.

If you decide you'd like to look into the possibility of getting a Newf from a rescue club, be prepared to answer a stringent questionnaire. The object of the club is to insure that the dog goes to the right home and is never again abandoned or given away.

Getting a dog from rescue can be a very rewarding and emotionally uplifting experience. Not only are you getting a wonderful friend and companion, but you'll also have the satisfaction of knowing you probably saved the dog's life. If you decide to open your heart to a rescue Newf, you will have to sign a spay/neuter contract. No matter what the quality of the dog—pet or show—the rescue club will not place it unless you agree to have it altered by an appointed time. Sometimes rescue dogs are already altered. There is a fee for adopting a rescue dog that goes back into the fund to help save other unfortunate Newfs.

The Newfoundland with Children

If, like most of us, you grew up enchanted by "Nana," the beloved, worry-wart Newf nanny of Wendy, Michael, and John in J. M. Barrie's *Peter Pan*, then you already have a good idea about the relationship between Newfs and children. The Newf is such a loyal companion and protector that in earlier times many families actually used the dogs to mind their small children. The Newf's devotion to youngsters is indeed legendary. Daring rescues have been recorded throughout the breed's history. Of all canines, the Newf is undoubtedly one of the best pets to have around children. Its natural protective instinct is a quality parents everywhere will appreciate. Despite its great size, the full-grown Newf is extremely gentle and nonaggressive with children. The two form an immediate bond and become fast friends and playmates for life. However, when bringing a Newf puppy into the house, as with any young dog, exercise care if there are children around. An energetic puppy will want to chase, play rough, and chew. Don't let your child become your new puppy's favorite toy—or vice versa. Both pup and child must be taught respect for each other. That way, by the time your Newf is a year old, it'll do just about everything but change your human baby's diapers!

The Newfoundland with Other Pets

The Newf is as loving and protective of other pets in the household as it is of its owners. A Newf raised with other pets has no problem adjusting. If you introduce another pet into the house once your Newf is older, it will probably be the other pet that will need to do the adjusting. Even to another dog, the Newf's great size can be intimidating. When bringing in another pet, introduce it to your Newf slowly. The Newf is a nonaggressive dog that accepts people and other pets with grace and generosity.

Despite its large size, it is very gentle with small pets. Many Newf owners with kittens report that their Newf takes over like a big "mama." As long as it doesn't perceive the newcomer as a threat to its loving family, the Newf will welcome a new arrival with open paws!

The Cost of Keeping a Newfoundland

Contrary to popular belief, it doesn't cost appreciably more money to own a Newf than, for example, an Irish setter. The largest financial investment you will make is the purchase price of your dog, which is comparable with most purebreds. You can expect to spend between $400 and $600 for a good pet-quality dog, somewhat more for a show dog. Other expenses are feeding, health care, and general maintenance. This will be the same for any dog you purchase, regardless of the breed.

True, a Newf will eat more than a Chihuahua, but just because the Newf weighs over 120 pounds (54 kg) as an adult, it doesn't mean it needs to eat tons of food. In fact, your Newf will eat appreciably less as it gets older. If you keep it on a high-quality, premium dog food, you will save money on veterinarian bills in the long run. Realistically, its monthly feeding bill will probably average about $40 to $60, depending on what supplements you add to its basic feed.

Regular veterinarian care should run about $200 per year, if the dog is healthy. One of the things you may want to look into is pet insurance. There are several companies that cover pets, as well as some companies that specialize in pet insurance. For a small premium per year, you can rest easy that, should your Newf require an expensive medical procedure, it will be covered.

Holiday Puppies

When the holidays roll around, it's often hard to resist the impulse to buy a puppy, tie a big bow around its neck, and put it under the Christmas tree. Word of advice? RESIST! You'll be glad you did. Again, use your common sense. The traditional portrait of Christmas, Hanukkah, and Easter may be tranquil, soothing, and benign, but the reality of any holiday never makes the cover of a greeting card. Holidays, while happy, festive times, are also chaotic, disruptive, and anything but orderly and quiet.

Don't bring a Newf pup into the house during the excitement and confusion of the holidays.

descend upon the house for some holiday cheer! Puppy, who has just arrived from the security and tranquillity of its breeder's kennel, is sure to suffer immediate culture shock. The normal excitement of the occasion will throw the new pup for a loop. All of the things you need when introducing a puppy into the house—consistency, patience, time—are out the window in a flash. How can you possibly see to your Newf's housetraining if you have to keep running into the kitchen to replenish drinks, make sure the kids aren't getting into the dessert, and check that the turkey isn't burning to a crisp? Do you really want your Newf to be a part of this picture? Do everyone a favor. WAIT. Get your puppy *after* the holidays when you'll have enough time to spend acclimating it to its new environment.

If you do purchase the puppy before the holidays, make sure you bring it home at least several weeks in advance. That way, it'll have its routine down and you'll have yours.

Incidentally, it's never a good idea to give a child a puppy for Christmas or any other occasion. While owning a dog can bring new meaning into the life of a child and create a bond of friendship that supersedes all others, a new pup is just that—a new addition to the household. It is not an object to be given and taken away like a windup toy, but rather a member of the family to be loved, respected, and cherished by all.

Imagine bringing a new puppy into the house on the same day that all 25 long-lost relatives of all ages and sizes

Living with Your Newfoundland

Before You Bring Your Newfoundland Home

Now that you have decided the Newfoundland is the right dog for you and have picked out your puppy from the breeder, you'll count the days until you can bring your cuddly bundle of joy home. Before you do, there are many preparations you'll have to make in anticipation of your pup's arrival. Make no mistake—planning for the arrival of a new dog is very much like bringing a new baby home. So put your thinking cap on and get to work!

First, you must realize that your new pet will need a period of adjustment to get used to its new surroundings. This is especially true if you bought an older dog. So expect a certain amount of apprehension and stress on its part for the first few days. The best way to make its transition easier is to have everything ready for it in its new home.

Food and Dishes. Before you pick up your Newf, your breeder will give you an idea of some basic supplies you'll need to have on hand. The first, of course, is food. Locate a good, full-service pet supply store in your area and get ready to stock up. Make sure the store carries the same brand of dog food your breeder has been using. Even if you decide to change the brand at a later date, it's wise to continue the diet the dog is used to for the first few months. While you're at the pet store, there are some other essential items you'll need to pick up, like dishes for food and water. Good heavy plastic or weighted stainless steel bowls are preferable because they won't slide around the floor. You may also want to purchase a raised stand for your Newf's bowls. There are many breeders who feel the dog accumulates less gas in its intestinal tract when it eats from a raised position.

Collar and Leash. Next, you'll need a collar and leash or lead. It's best to purchase one permanent collar, either leather or nylon, which your Newf will wear all of the time with its identification tag attached. You should also purchase a choke or a "slip" collar for use when your walk your Newf on the leash. Don't be upset by the word *choke*. When used properly, the collar does not choke the dog, but only gives its neck enough of a tug to get its attention. Never leave a choke collar on your dog when not on a leash.

Use a metal or nylon choke collar for training. Once the training session is over, remove the choker and replace it with a buckle or snap collar.

HOW-TO:
Newf-Proofing Your Home

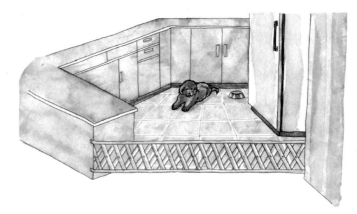

Once you have all the supplies your Newf will need, the next thing you'll have to do is get your house ready for its arrival.

• If you have cabinets in your kitchen or elsewhere in the house, you should "child-proof" them with appropriate locks. Your veterinarian can advise you on the best choices. Puppies, like babies, have a genius for getting into forbidden places.

• If you have stairs in your home, you may want to section them off from your pup with a gate.

• Make sure decks and balconies are also closed off.

• Remove all objects and bric-a-brac from tables or counters that are accessible to the puppy.

• Remove all electrical cords from any area your Newf will have access to. While your puppy is teething, it will seize on almost anything to satisfy its chewing urge. Chewing on an electrical cord could shock or even kill it.

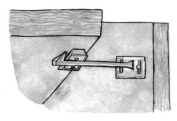

Keep your Newf pup out of places like the kitchen cabinets by installing "child-proof" locks.

Section off part of a room, preferably the kitchen, so your puppy will have its own special place for quiet time.

• Remove any toxic plants from your home and yard. Your veterinarian and/or local nursery can provide you with a list of poisonous house and yard plants.

• Section off a portion of a room, usually the kitchen, for your Newf until it is acclimated to its new surroundings and is completely housebroken. Having its own space will give the dog more confidence and you fewer headaches.

If you want to keep your Newf outdoors part of the time, you should have a fenced-in yard or kennel area. If you plan to leave it out for any amount of time, be sure it has shelter from the elements. You can purchase an all-weather doghouse at your pet store for this purpose or build one yourself. If you do construct your own house, make sure it is big enough to accommodate a full-sized Newf and that it is properly insulated. Your pet store also sells various types of pet doors that can be attached to the door of the house, allowing

your Newf to let itself in and out at will. However, if you use a pet door, it should always lead into a completely fenced yard or kennel area. Never let your pet door lead out to an open area or street.

The day before you bring your Newf home, it's a good idea to gather family members together and have a conference about the do's and don'ts once your Newf arrives. Make sure everyone knows what is expected of them. The best way to be sure that your Newf will acclimate to its new surroundings is for everyone to help out and make the transition a happy one.

When you Newf-proof your home, be sure to remove any wires from electrical sockets within the pup's reach.

Before bringing your puppy home, be sure to purchase a nylon or leather leash and be sure you have a permanent identification tag attached to its everyday collar.

Because of the *slip* nature of the choke collar, it can easily become hooked onto another object and cause serious injury to your dog. The choke allows you to correct your dog instantly when it pulls or lunges.

If you have a puppy, remember it will soon grow out of the collar. To maximize your investment, choose one with ample room for expansion as the pup's neck grows. Next, pick a sturdy six-foot (2 m) leash in either nylon or leather. (Nylon tends to wear better.) Your pet store will also have several types of identification tags available. You can fill out an order form with your pet's name and your address and phone number. In approximately one to two weeks, you'll receive the tag in the mail.

Toys. If you're like most new pet owners, you'll also want to have some toys ready for your new pet to play with. If you have a puppy, remember it will need to satisfy its chewing urge, so purchase toys with that in mind. There are many good, sturdy nylon toys available that will not only keep it from teething on the leg of your dining room table, but will give the dog hours of pleasure as well. These toys have the added benefit of massaging the gums and, consequently, will make the pup feel good, too. Various types of rawhide chews are also satisfactory.

Your Newfoundland's First Night in Your Home

The moment you've been waiting for has arrived. You finally have your beautiful Newf home with you. A puppy will be naturally excited and active in its new surroundings. It will want to play and do lots of exploring. If you have already pet-proofed your home, there's no danger that your Newf will get into trouble. If there are children in the family, be sure they know their responsibility where the new pup is concerned. Don't allow children to manhandle the puppy, pulling at its tail or ears. They should respect it as they would any member of the household.

Once your pup has had a few minutes of play and introduction to the rest of the family, take it outside to the special spot you have designated and allow it to relieve itself. Remember, puppies will need to go out after they play or become excited. Don't let your Newf become overexcited on its first day home. After it has had its play session and you've taken it out, put it in its special area, whether that's a crate or a portion of a room you've sectioned off, and allow the dog to take a nap. Puppies need their sleep. Your Newf will also need to know it has a spot all its own where it can go and have some quiet time. It should have its own bed or mat and several toys like nylon bones that it can chew on when it awakens. Don't be upset if it cries or whimpers when it's left alone. This is normal. Until the puppy gets used to having its own space, it will cry to be with you. Don't give into its pitiful wails by constantly going over to soothe it or, worse, by allowing it to be with you. If you do, you will be laying the groundwork for unwanted behavior in the future, teaching it that every time it cries, you'll come running. Be gentle but firm, and above all, consistent.

Put several layers of clean newspaper down in your puppy's pen or section of the house, in case it needs to eliminate when you are not at home.

After you've taken your Newf out for the last time in the evening, put it in its special spot to sleep. Be sure to leave some newspapers spread out in case it needs to relieve itself during the night. Again, it may cry, but don't worry. Your Newf will soon calm

Teach your puppy to eliminate outside by taking it out to the same spot several times a day, especially after meals and naps.

down and fall asleep. If it really seems upset, you can try leaving on a radio or a cassette tape playing soft music. Usually, the sound of voices or soft melodies will soon lull it to sleep. Remember, don't give into its whining, no matter how pitiful it sounds. It goes without saying that you should be able to distinguish between whining for attention and a serious distress cry or yelp. Let common sense be your best guide.

Housebreaking Your Newfoundland

When you bring your Newf home, the first thing you'll want to take care of is housebreaking the pup. Once you begin your regular training exercises, you'll realize your puppy will be anxious to please you. The same goes for getting the hang of housebreaking.
• Let your puppy know *where* you want it to eliminate and *when*. But remember, a puppy has to relieve itself much more often than an adult dog, so be patient.
• Take your pup out as soon as it awakens from a nap and after each meal or exercise period.
• Take it out again just before you go to bed. Soon it will associate going out with the pleasurable experience of relieving itself.
• When it does eliminate in the proper place, praise it profusely. Remember, however, that accidents will happen no matter how consistent you try to be. Patience is essential.
• *Never* rub your pup's nose in its excrement or use a rolled up newspaper to correct it. Simply clean up the mess and bring it to the place where you want it to eliminate and praise it. It'll soon get the idea.

You can help the housebreaking process by feeding your Newf at regular times each day and then walking it directly afterward.

A well-trained Newfoundland is a loyal and devoted companion to its human master.

Traveling with Your Newfoundland

When flying with your Newf, always remove its collar before locking it in an airline carrier. Be sure its identification and destination are clearly written on the outside of the carrier.

Car Travel

Some owners decide to take their pets with them on trips. If you do, make your plans well in advance. If traveling by car, you'll need a safe place for your Newf to stay while you do the driving. A crate is very helpful in this situation. It's safer for the dog and for you. An unrestrained animal in a moving vehicle is an accident waiting to happen. If you don't want to use a crate, you can also purchase a suitable pet gate that can effectively section off the back seat of the car from the front.

If you have the car windows open, don't allow your dog to stick its head out. Flying debris from the road can hit it and cause damage, especially to its eyes.

Remember never to leave your pet in the car in warm weather. Even if you open the windows, the inside of the car can become like an inferno in direct sunlight light in just a few minutes.

If you travel with your Newfoundland, be sure to have a crate of appropriate size on hand. As a safety precaution, a dog should always be crated when traveling in a car.

Before you start out, find out which motels allow pets. Most major hotel/motel chains publish booklets, listing their various locations all over the country along with a note advising whether pets are allowed at a particular spot. Auto clubs and travel guides can also be of assistance.

Air Travel

• If you travel by plane with your pet, find out the rules and regulations regarding pets for the airline you will be using. Airlines require an approved carrier as well as health certificates for your pet. Be sure your Newf is up-to-date on all of its vaccinations.
• Always travel on the same flight as your pet to avoid its being accidentally shipped to another destination. On the day of departure, arrive at the airport with lots of time to spare so you can see that your Newf is handled properly and not rushed through the boarding process.
• Make sure it has been allowed to relieve itself before it's loaded onto the plane. Your pet will have to ride in a specially pressurized section of the baggage compartment that is fully air-conditioned.
• When you board the plane, it's a good idea to remind the flight attendant that your Newf is traveling with you, and ask him or her to inform the pilot. The

flight crew is told before takeoff when there are pets on board, but it doesn't hurt to remind them, just for safety's sake.
• Don't put your Newf into its carrier with a choke chain around its neck. In fact, it's best to remove all collars and tape its identification information on the outside of the carrier along with your name, destination, phone and flight number.
• Also stick "Live Animal" decals in a prominent place on the carrier.
• Don't put any food inside, but do attach the airline conversion kit that comes with the airline carrier. This will permit your dog to have water available. Make certain the door of the carrier is fastened correctly and locked.
• If your pet is a good traveler, it should have no ill effects on the trip. However, some animals experience motion sickness or are just very nervous travelers. Ask your veterinarian's advice before you leave. He or she may want to prescribe motion sickness medicine or a mild tranquilizer to make the pet's trip less stressful.

Finally, before leaving, double check if the hotel or motel where you will be staying is expecting your pet. There is generally a daily minimal charge. If you're visiting friends or family members, advise them you are bringing your Newf along and make sure they are agreeable.

Home Alone

If the puppy is alone all or part of the day, don't give it the run of the house. A pup needs boundaries or its life will seem very confusing. Some people like to section off a part of a room, preferably the kitchen or laundry room.

• Leave clean newspapers down each time you go out, and let your Newf become accustomed to eliminating on the papers when you're not there to take it outside.

• Some owners prefer to use a crate to keep their pup in line while they are away from the house. If you do use a crate, consider purchasing the largest size available. That way, you will be able to use it later when your Newf is full grown, should you need to confine it for brief periods.

• If you have a large enough crate, section off a part of it for the pup's elimination needs. However, never leave your pup in a crate for more than four or five hours at a time.

• A puppy pen is another good way to keep your Newf out of trouble and still give it some space. Puppy pens can be purchased at pet stores or from wholesale pet catalogs. You can also make one yourself. Like the crate, the object of the puppy pen is to give your pet boundaries and a sense of security in its new environment.

Be aware that your Newf will need lots of exercise, but don't overdo it. Puppies tend to run out of gas fast. Always follow up play/exercise sessions with a quick trip outside so the puppy can relieve itself. Then put it down for a nap.

Boarding Your Newfoundland

When it comes time for you to take a few days off or go on a family vacation, you'll have to decide what arrangements you will make for your Newf.

If you're like most people, you'll probably want to send your Newf on a vacation of its own while you take yours. There are many reputable boarding kennels where your Newf can stay while you're away. If they are accredited with the American Boarding Kennel Association (ABKA), all the better. However, many non-ABKA kennels are also excellent. The best way to be sure your Newf will spend a safe and pleasant time away from you is to check out the facilities in your area and plan to visit several of them beforehand. When choosing a boarding kennel, make sure the establishment has large indoor and outdoor runs that are kept meticulously clean and odor-free. The kennel should also have a large exercise area where your Newf can have its play time each day while you're away. Be sure your pet will get individualized attention and that the kennel has a good ratio of professional attendants to the number of animals being boarded. Also make sure the kennel has a veterinarian on call 24 hours a day, in the event of emergency. As another safety precaution, make sure the kennel is equipped with heat and smoke alarms and an automatic sprinkler system. There should be someone in attendance 24 hours a day. Don't be shy about asking all of these questions. The only way for your Newf to be safe and happy while you're away is for you to find it the best kennel possible. A reputable kennel will be proud of its reputation and happy to answer any questions or reservations you may have.

If you choose to board your pet, be aware the cost may be high. Quality kennels are not cheap, but whatever the price, it's a small one to pay for peace of mind. Don't bargain hunt when selecting a kennel. Your Newf's safety depends on your making the best choice possible.

When you leave your Newf at the kennel for its "vacation," remember to bring along its food; otherwise, the

A young puppy needs boundaries and should never be given the complete run of the house when you are away.

keep its diet consistent. Leave written instructions regarding when to feed, the amount to feed, and any supplements or medications that need to be given as well. Be sure to bring some of your Newf's favorite toys so it will feel almost right at home. A favorite blanket or even an old coat of yours to use as bedding may make your pet feel more at home. Be sure to leave the name and phone number of your veterinarian in case any health problems crop up. You should also leave a number where you can be reached in an emergency.

If you prefer not to put your Newf in a kennel while you're away, you might want to consider a pet-sitting service. Your veterinarian may be able to recommend people who either take pets into their homes and watch them while the owner is away or pet-sitters who will stay with your pet in your home. If you answer an ad in the newspaper for a pet-sitter, be sure to interview the person beforehand and demand to see references and then call the people on the list.

Of course, all of the above may be unnecessary if you have a willing friend or relative who will watch your Newf while you're on vacation. This is another reason to have a set of good "doggy" friends who all pitch in to help each other in times just like this.

kennel attendants will feed it whatever brand of feed they generally use. Since this will be an initially stressful time for your pet, the best way to avoid stressing its system further is to

Training Your Newfoundland

The Basic Premise of Training

In order to appreciate the whole concept of training, it's important to understand the order of the canine world. Like its fellow canine, the wolf, the dog is essentially a pack animal. In its world, there is a clearly defined hierarchy that determines its actions from puppyhood. In the wild, a dog's place in the pack is determined by its strength. The top or "alpha" dog is the strongest and most aggressive male. It sets the rules and doles out the punishment whenever another dog gets out of line. It is the leader until it is displaced by another, stronger male.

Though our domestic dogs are far removed from their ancestral packs, they instinctively understand the pack order. When a pup is born, its mother acts as top dog. She rewards its good behavior and corrects its bad behavior. Once the puppy leaves its mother, you will have to assume the role of "top dog." Your Newf expects you to establish order in its world. The way to do that is by training it to please you. Far from being harsh or cruel, training your dog is the best thing you can do for it. It will make its world and yours a much happier and tranquil place.

Getting Started

Getting your mind set into the training mode isn't easy. How can it be when all you can see in front of you is a cute, cuddly Newfy pup? Everything it does, including jumping on you for love and attention and nibbling at your arms and feet with its razor-sharp milk teeth, is too endearing to stop. In fact, it's so adorable, you simply can't say "No" to it. Think again and project a year into the future when your bouncing 15-pounder (6.8 kg) is tipping the scales at well over 100 pounds (45 kg)! How cute will it be then when it wants your attention and ends up knocking you down and sending you straight to the local chiropractor? As the old adage goes, an ounce of prevention is worth a pound of cure. Simple translation: learn to say "No" from Day One, and a year later you'll have a well-adjusted, happy dog that is a pleasure to live with. Far from being a negative expression, the training process is very positive and something you and your Newf can enjoy together. It will serve as the basis of

Left drawing: the correct position for a choke collar. Right drawing: the wrong position for a choke collar.

The choke collar correctly positioned, should resemble the letter "P" when held directly in front of you. Left drawing: correct position. Right drawing: wrong position

your teamwork and mutual cooperation throughout your lives together. So pick up that collar and leash and prepare to have some fun.

The first rule of training is consistency. Remember the mother dog. When the pup got too sassy, Mother corrected it immediately, every time,

Hold the choke collar in front of your Newf and let it form the letter "P," then slip it over the dog's head.

not just now and then. So don't reprimand your Newf three times for jumping on the couch and then let it get away with it the fourth time. Be consistent, just like the mother dog. That way, your pup will understand what you expect of it. Use your tone of voice to tell it which behavior is permitted and which is not. When it jumps on the couch, assuming you don't want it on the furniture, say "No" firmly, then scoop it into a sitting position on the floor and praise it immediately. *Always* follow a correction with praise for the desired behavior. This will not confuse your Newf. Instead, your tone of voice will let it know what you want of it. However, don't expect it to get it right the first time—training requires *repetition* and *patience*.

Crate Training

There are pros and cons to using a crate. Certainly no dog should be kept exclusively in a crate. However, when used properly, you'll find the crate has several advantages. First and foremost, it will keep your pup from getting into things like kitchen cabinets and drawers whenever you're out of the house. Not only is it annoying to come home and find the house a shambles, but your pup can also injure itself. If it is trained to stay in a crate while you're away, it will soon come to regard the space as its den and will actually look forward to its "private" time inside the crate. It will even retreat there during the day when it wants its own space. The size of the crate depends on the size of the dog. Since the Newf will grow to a formidable stature, you may want to start off with a crate it will be able to use throughout its life. A dog should always be able to stand to its full height and be able to turn and change position in a crate. Never use the crate as a punishment for unacceptable behavior. Your pup should feel

34

that its crate is its refuge from the rough and tumble of daily life.

Acclimate your pup to the crate as soon as it arrives in its new home. Most pups come with crate experience, since breeders almost always keep their litters crated. If your pup has been crated before, that will make your job all the easier. If your Newf is not accustomed to being in a crate, introduce it slowly, with gradually longer periods of time. After play, put it in its crate for a nap. You may want to put down a mat or towel on the bottom of the crate and include one or two of its toys, just to make it feel at home. When it awakens, take it outside to relieve itself. Play with your pup for a few moments and then put it back into its crate while you go about your household chores. If it barks or cries, look it straight in the eye and firmly tell it "No." When you travel with your pet, the crate will also come in handy. If you own a van or station wagon, simply set up the crate in the rear area, lock your Newf in, and buckle up your seat belts. You're ready to roll. The crate is a safety device for your pet whenever it travels with you in the car. It will also prevent it from jumping all over you and distracting you, possibly causing an accident while you're trying to drive.

Collar and Leash Training

Get your Newf used to a collar and leash as soon as you pick it up from the breeder. For its own safety and the safety of others, a dog should never be allowed to roam freely so start developing good habits from the outset. Initially, your pup may resist both collar and leash, unless the breeder has already accustomed it to accept one or both. In any case, it will soon get the hang of it. For everyday wear, your Newf should have a snap-on or buckle-down collar with its identification and rabies tags attached.

To teach your Newf to sit, hold the leash securely in your right hand and press gently on the backs of its legs with the left hand, repeating the command "sit."

For training purposes, use a thin metal or nylon choke collar. Remove it immediately after the training session is complete. Use a six-foot (2 m) leash or lead of approximately ¾ inch–1 inch (2–2.5 cm) wide. Take some time to get your Newf used to both the collar and the lead so it won't be afraid of it. Let it wear the collar and drag the lead for a few minutes so it can get the feel of it. When you pick up the other end of the lead, the pup will tug and resist. Don't allow yourself to be pulled in the direction it wants to go. Simply stand still as it pulls and tugs. Say "No," then give your lead a quick jerk, bringing the puppy to your side. Sit it down and praise it. Now you're ready for basic obedience.

HOW-TO:
Teaching Your Newfoundland to Heel

Now it's time to teach your Newf to let you take him for a walk rather than vice versa. We've all seen hapless owners holding onto a lead for dear life while their pet lunges and pushes ahead, literally taking *them* for a jog. Imagine this scenario with an adult Newf who weighs over 100 pounds (45 kg)! It's not only bad behavior, but it's also dangerous for you and your dog. Think about the possible repercussions. You could fall and be injured (especially in icy, slippery conditions), or your dog could break away, get hit by a car, or attack another dog or pedestrian. Not

When you stop walking, put your Newf into a "sit" position immediately. Then tell it to "stay." After you complete the exercise, begin it again.

a pretty picture, by any stretch of the imagination. Teaching your Newf to walk beside you will make your daily outings a pleasure for the both of you.

Begin by putting the choke collar and lead on your dog. By now your Newf already associates this practice with its training sessions and hopefully with having fun because it is pleasing you. Assume your regular starting position with your Newf on your left side. Hold the loop end of your lead in the right hand and begin walking. Your Newf will probably forge ahead. When it comes to the end of its lead space, stop walking. This will bring it to an abrupt stop as well. Now begin walking again. The same pattern will undoubtedly repeat itself. Your Newf will look at you, confused—"What did I do wrong?" Tell your dog to sit and then walk up to him,

To teach your Newf to "heel," stand on its right side and put it into a "sit" position. Gently tug on the slack in the leash and say "heel" and begin walking.

When your Newf has successfully completed the exercise, praise him lavishly.

coming to a halt when he is on your left side. Pick up the slack of the lead in your left hand and with a short tug of the left hand say, "Thunder, heel." Immediately take a step with your left foot. Your Newf should get up and follow. If he does not, tug on the lead again. Now you're holding the lead in both hands, the looped end in the right, the slack in the left. When he tries to get ahead of you, use the left hand to tug on the lead, repeating, "Thunder, heel." Don't stop walking; simply repeat the correction and command each time he tries to pull ahead. The object is to have his head in line with your left leg. Once you have him heeling, stop and tell him to sit. Praise him and repeat the exercise again. As your Newf becomes more familiar with the exercise, he will learn to sit automatically each time you come to a stop.

If you are having trouble getting your Newf to heel, trying coaxing him with a treat.

The ultimate objective of the heeling exercise is to train your Newf to heel off the lead. If you decide to pursue an obedience championship with your Newf, he will have to complete all the above exercises off lead. However, for everyday pur- poses, the heeling command is helpful to keep your Newf in line when you take him on his daily walks on the lead.

Basic obedience training will make your life and your Newf's more manageable and enjoyable.

Basic Obedience Training

Besides love and affection, one of the most important things you will impart to your precious Newf is basic obedience training. It could save its life and make yours a lot easier. Since the Newf is a working dog, it instinctively adapts well to obedience training. Many schools and communities offer formal obedience classes in various levels of difficulty. Generally, dogs under six months of age are not accepted. An alternative for the young pup is something called "puppy kinder-garten," the canine version of nursery school for your baby. Basically, puppy kindergarten is a means of socializing your puppy and getting it started on some basic commands. However, you can start it on basic commands your-self. Even if you enroll it in puppy kindergarten, you should also work with it every day yourself to reinforce what it has learned. Puppies have short attention spans and learn by constant repetition. Remember, there

If you have trouble putting your Newf into a "sit" position, gently pressing down on its rear usually does the trick.

are two cardinal rules in obedience training: be consistent and make it fun. Okay, let's get started!

Sitting on Command

Anyone who has ever had a dog who leaps and jumps and twirls when visitors arrive, can appreciate the need to have "Thunder" sit on command. Begin by slipping on his choke collar and leash. Bring him to a standing position with you on his right side. He will be on your left side. Always begin training sessions by assuming this starting position. Holding the leash in your right hand, pull back slightly. Simultaneously, press the backs of your Newf's legs behind the knee area with your left hand. This will make his legs buckle and he will ease into a "sit" position. At the same time, say, "Thunder, sit." As soon as your Newf is sitting, praise him. Repeat the exercise about five times at each session. If you work with him every day, after a few days your Newf will understand what you want and will be sitting on command. The better he gets, the more praise you should lavish on him. If your pup is resistant, try using a treat. Instead of using the leash and choker, simply hold a treat in front and above his head with your right hand and press into the backs of his legs as before while saying, "Thunder, sit." When he obeys, give him the treat instantly, while praising him—"Good boy!" When your pup masters the exercise, remove the treat and get him used to sitting on command just for the praise that follows.

The Sit/Stay Command

Once your Newf has mastered the art of the "sit" command, it's time to get him to "stay" in that position until you tell him otherwise. Begin this exercise by repeating the "sit" exercise above. Remember, you are holding the lead in your right hand. Once the dog sits, quickly pass your left palm in front of his

Once your pup is in a "sit" position, pass your left hand across its face and tell it to "stay." Then step in front and face your Newf. If it gets up, return it to the "sit" position and repeat the command "stay."

nose and say, "Thunder, stay." Then, still holding the lead, step in front of him. If he gets up, quickly return him to the "sit" position, pass your left palm in front of his nose, and repeat, "Stay." After several repetitions, he'll figure

Sit/stay is one of the most important commands your Newf will master. Follow correct performance with lavish praise.

Coax your Newf into the "down" position by getting it into a "sit" position and gently tugging downward on the leash, while saying "down."

out what you want him to do. Once your Newf stays on command, walk around his right side and return to the starting position on his left side. Then bend down and praise him. If at any time he breaks the stay, simply return him to the sitting position and repeat the "stay" command until it gets it right and you are able to return to the starting position.

Coming on Command

One of the biggest frustrations in a dog owner's life is having a pet ignore you when you ask him to come. Here's how to rectify that. Using your choke collar and lead, allow your Newf to go to the full length of the lead, then call him—"Thunder, come." As you do so, give a tug on the lead and begin reeling him in toward you, as if you were reeling in a fish on a line. When your Newf approaches you, quickly praise him. After four or five sessions, he should come without your having to reel him in. Then add another step to the exercise. When your Newf comes on command, tell him to "sit" when he

approaches you. As in the basic "sit" command, if your pup is resistant, you can also try the treat method. When the dog comes successfully, reward him with an enthusiastic "Good Boy" and a treat. Then add the "sit" command as above.

The "Down" Command

Now that you're beginning to feel good about the progress you're making, let's add another command to your Newf's basic repertoire. Lying down is a fairly natural position for a dog, but it's probably one of the hardest things to get your pet to do, especially if you've waited until he's an adult to get started with obedience work. If you get your Newf as a pup, teach him the "down" and "down/stay" exercise early on. You won't regret your efforts.

Again, begin with your Newf on your left side. Command him to sit. If you need to press on the backs of his legs with your left hand, do so. Then with the lead in your right hand, gently tug straight down while saying, "Thunder, down." If this doesn't work, try the treat method. Once Thunder is sitting, hold the treat below his nose and say, "Thunder, down," while lowering the treat to floor level, until the dog must get down on all fours to get it. When he does, praise him.

Once your Newf has mastered these four basic commands inside the house, it's time to try them outdoors where there will be many more distractions. Remember, be patient, be consistent, and you will succeed!

Obedience Classes

Enrolling your Newf in a formal group obedience class is a rewarding and challenging experience for both dog and owner. Many local dog clubs run classes several times a year. The purpose of the classes is not only to train your dog but to train you as well. Getting together once a week with other dog owners will boost your confidence and give you a chance to share and compare your experiences. If you've been working with your Newf religiously on his basic obedience, you'll probably be the star of the class! Remember, if you plan to enjoy other Newfy activities like backpacking, water trials, and tracking, obedience training is essential. You and your Newf must learn to work as a team, and enrolling in a novice obedience class is the best way to start. There are also private classes that are given by professional trainers, but, generally speaking, a group class is preferable because it gets your dog and you used to distractions and other dogs. The group class is also a great way to socialize a shy pup and work on problem areas with an overly enthusiastic Newf. You may find that you and your Newf enjoy obedience work so much that you'll decide to continue and pursue an obedience title.

The Newfoundland in Obedience Trials

The American Kennel Club first established obedience trials in the 1930s. The purpose of the competition, which has three levels or classes of increasing difficulty, is to determine the dog's ability to obey a set of commands while accomplishing a set of tasks. There are four different obedience titles awarded when the dog has successfully completed a class:

1. The CD title (Companion Dog) is awarded to a dog in the novice class.

2. The CDX (Companion Dog Excellent) is awarded to a dog in the open class.

3. The UD (Utility Dog) is awarded to a dog in the utility class.

4. The OTCH (Obedience Trial Championship) is the highest obedience title a dog can win.

The competitions consist of high and broad jumps, retrieving, scent

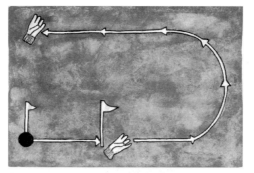

Before a tracking event begins, a tracklayer walks the course and drops an object he has been carrying that the dog must later find.

discrimination, and a series of "stay" and "sit" commands.

To date, there have been only two Newfoundlands who have been awarded an OTCH. The first was OTCH Barbara Allen's Jessie, WD (Water Dog) in 1982 and the second was OTCH Sweetbay's Gretl, TD (Tracking Dog). Gretl was also the first Newfy to ever achieve a perfect score of 200! When Gretl retired from competition in 1991, she was given a special award for outstanding achievement.

The handler harnesses the dog to a 30–40 foot lead and starts it at the beginning of the track, pointing to the ground so it can pick up the scent.

The Newfoundland excels in obedience trials. Working with your Newf toward an obedience title can be both rewarding and great fun.

The Newfoundland as a Working Dog

One of the characteristics that sets the Newfoundland apart from other breeds is its prowess as a working dog. In today's computer age, we don't think much about a dog having

In earlier times, one of the Newfoundland's chief functions was as a carting and hauling dog. Today, many owners continue to train their Newfs to haul heavy loads.

a specific task to perform, except perhaps for those canines trained as guide dogs for the blind. Yet, in earlier times, as we've already mentioned, a dog's worth was judged specifically by its ability to be a working member of the household. In short, it had to pull its own weight. That's why the Newf, due to its great size and placid disposition, gained acceptance as a working member of the family.

In contemporary society, we don't ask our canine companions to do much more than fetch a newspaper or roll over. Nonetheless, the Newf is still occasionally called upon by its master to assist in some of the labors of daily living. Teams of Newfs were running mail to remote outposts in their native Newfoundland until the 1940s. Today, however, Newfs also provide valuable assistance as search-and-rescue dogs. Since most Newf owners want to preserve the breed's working characteristics, they allow their dogs to compete in water, rescue, tracking, and draft trials as developed by the Newfoundland Club of America. These events not only provide the dog an opportunity to do what it was bred to do, but also give Newf owners a chance to socialize and enjoy fun family activities with their dogs.

Water Tests

The Newfoundland's natural swimming ability and stamina in the water make it the ideal water rescue dog. In fact, you could call it a canine lifeguard. Its instinct is to jump into the water and aid anyone or anything in distress. Thus, the object of the water training and later, the water test, is to team up owner and dog in a number of exercises to demonstrate obedience and ability to perform the task of retrieve and rescue.

Before you take your Newf to any of the dozen water tests across the country sanctioned by the Newfoundland

The water test teams up dog and owner in a variety of exercises to demonstrate obedience and the dog's ability to perform the task of retrieve and rescue.

In one exercise, the handler must drop an object into at least 2 feet of water and command the dog to "get it."

In another exercise, the handler will get into the water and cry for help. The Newfoundland must then jump in after her and pull her to safety.

Club of America each year, you will first have to train it in basic obedience and then introduce it to the water. It will adapt to both easily and with flair. Start your Newf out from puppyhood. One of the first instructions it will have to master is to come on command.

When you and your Newf participate in water tests, you do so as a team. You are the team leader; therefore, you must be in complete control of your dog. Your Newf will have to learn things like the retrieve and delivery. It will have to learn to hold and then give, to pull and carry, all of which are designed to teach it to rescue.

Training your Newf to take part in water tests is hard but rewarding work for both of you. Dogs who qualify in the Junior Division of the water trial are awarded the title WD (Water Dog). Those successfully competing in the Senior Division are awarded the title WRD (Water Rescue Dog).

Carting and Hauling

When you see a full-grown adult Newf, it is easy to understand why it was worth its weight in gold as a carting and hauling dog. Its size plus its massive musculature made it perfect for hauling heavy loads. At the turn of the century, Newfs commonly worked in harness for their masters. While their hauling activities today may be restricted to pulling a wagon full of toddlers around a playground, taking the children for a sleigh ride after the first snowfall, or dragging a freshly cut Christmas tree into the house, properly trained Newfs perform all these activities with willingness and enthusiasm.

Before you harness up your Newf to the family sled, it will have to be obedience trained. As in water training, carting and hauling demands a dog that is under its master's control at all times. Introduce your Newf to a harness slowly; otherwise it may resist and panic, and what could have been a fun activity for all will be ruined. Don't begin to harness train your Newf until it is physically mature. Young puppies have not had enough time to develop and could be injured if harnessed too soon.

Carting and hauling requires great stamina and conditioning, so you will have to gradually start extending your Newf's exercise periods for longer intervals to build up its muscles and endurance. One of the best ways to accomplish this is to swim your Newf.

Swimming builds up muscles better than any other type of exercise and is also something the dog will enjoy.

Jogging

Jogging on a soft surface is also an excellent endurance exercise and something you can do with your pet so you can both stay in shape. Although many people like to exercise their dogs while riding a bicycle, this is not advisable. The dog could easily pull the wrong way or go too fast and you could both be seriously injured. Furthermore, you could inadvertently topple into the path of an oncoming car.

Roadworking

Roadworking, or attaching your Newf with a lead to the back bumper of your car is also not recommended. It's very difficult to maintain a slow speed for a long, steady interval and roadworking is dangerous. Imagine having to hit the brake suddenly and having your Newf come crashing into the rear end of the car, or under it!

If you do decide to train your Newf for hauling and carting, you can have fun by entering draft test competitions. The purpose of these competitions is to demonstrate the Newf's ability to perform these skills in real work situations. There are two different draft titles your dog can earn: Draft Dog (DD), which is awarded to dogs competing individually, or Team Draft Dog (TDD), awarded to teams of two or more dogs working together. In order to qualify, your Newf must show a willingness to be harnessed and hitched, and then demonstrate obedience to commands while it successfully maneuvers a cart. Finally, it must pull a load over a course of at least one mile.

While preparing your Newf for draft competition isn't easy, like the water trials, it is a rewarding experience and one that will strengthen the bond between you and your dog.

Tracking

If you've ever seen an old movie where the local lawmen were trudging through the swamps with a bunch of bloodhounds in tow, you get the basic idea of what tracking is all about. Tracking, which is an AKC-recognized sport, requires the dog to track a human scent over a specific course. In this type of event, both dog and owner work as a team to locate a specific human scent left by a "tracklayer."

The competition begins with a *track* mapped out over a course of approximately 500 yards (457 m) and divided into two sections with corners. The tracklayer plants a flag into the ground at the beginning of the course and then begins walking it through as specified by the judge. At the 30-yard (27 m) mark, the tracklayer plants another flag and continues to the end of the course. When the tracklayer reaches the end, he or she drops an object that he or she has been carrying throughout the course—a glove, a wallet, a shoe. It is then up to the dog to navigate the course and find the object containing the scent. The handler will start the dog, who is harnessed to a 30- to 40-foot (9–12 m) lead, at the first flag. The handler then indicates the spot so the dog can pick up the scent. The dog, nose to ground, then moves forward, following the scent path. If the dog makes it to the second flag, the handler will know the dog has the scent and will continue to follow wherever the dog leads until the object is found. If the Newf finds the object, it passes the test and earns the title of Tracking Dog (TD).

It is interesting to point out that in tracking, your Newf will really be on its own. You, the handler, simply hold onto the lead and follow where the dog takes you. You cannot correct the dog or use any of the other obedience commands that were essential in all of the other activities. Tracking requires the dog to operate on an instinctual level.

Backpacking

One of the most rewarding activities you can enjoy with your Newf is backpacking. There's nothing like a hike in the woods or a camping trip in the mountains when all of nature is in bloom—and no one will enjoy accompanying you more than your Newf. Not only will it help haul your gear, but it'll be at your side at all times. However, before you take your Newf out on the trail, it must be trained to obey your commands. There are many distractions out in the woods, from other animals to fellow travelers, and an unruly dog will prove a menace to itself and anyone else in its path.

When you get ready to hit the trails with your Newf, be sure its backpack is well balanced. Even though it is a working dog and loves to be challenged with a task, it shouldn't be weighted down with too heavy a load. In short, don't allow your Newf to tote your camping gear, food, pots and pans, and anything else in sight. Use common sense and prepare to have a great time.

One of the fun activities you and your Newf can do together is backpacking in the great outdoors.

On some beaches on the Italian Riviera, Newfoundland rescue dogs are members of the lifeguard team.

Since hauling heavy loads requires great strength and stamina, you will have to get your Newf into condition gradually, exercising it to build up its muscles.

Feeding Your Newfoundland

A Balanced Diet

There are few subjects that invite as heated a debate as the type of food to feed your dog. Everyone seems to have an opinion on what to feed, how much, and how often. Beyond all the rhetoric and attractive dog food labels, the bottom line is a simple one: feed your Newf a balanced diet—one that is rich in high-quality protein, carbohydrates, fats, vitamins, and minerals. This will help build strong bones and muscles and generally keep it in good, healthy condition. In order for a diet to be balanced, all of these components must be present.

Choosing the Right Dog Food

There are many dog foods on the market available through a variety of retail and specialty stores. Despite the attractive labeling and extensive advertising in the media, all commercial dog foods are not equal. Don't purchase one just because the ad appealed to you. When choosing a feed for your Newf, be judicious.
• Read the label and go over the list of ingredients.
• Pay particular attention to the first three or four ingredients listed. They make up the greatest proportion of the food. The rest of the ingredients will not significantly affect the nutritional content.
• Buy a good premium dog food. It will supply all the daily requirements your Newf will need. A premium food may be more expensive, but it will save you money in the end. Because of the high quality of ingredients in premium

foods, you can expect to feed your dog less of it. Unlike many commercial feeds, premium food will not contain "filler" ingredients designed to add bulk rather than nutrition to the feed. Premium foods will have far fewer and more easily understood ingredient lists than other commercial foods. The companies that manufacture premium foods usually have hard research data to back up their nutritional claims.
• If you know your dog has a particular health problem, such as a food allergy, keep that in mind when purchasing a food. For example, some dogs cannot tolerate foods that contain soy, wheat, or corn. They may vomit, have diarrhea, scratch, or exhibit other symptoms. But these are individual sensitivities and you should be able to

There are three different types of dog food: dry, canned, and semi-moist.

Puppy Feeding Plan

8–12 weeks: 4 meals a day

Morning: ½ cup of dry puppy food mixed with a little warm water.

Noon: ½ cup of dry puppy food.

Evening: ½ cup of dry puppy food mixed with a little warm water.

Bedtime: ½ cup of dry puppy food.

10–12 weeks: 3 meals a day

Morning: 1½ cups of puppy food mixed with a little water and any supplement recommended by your breeder.

Noon: 1½ cups of dry puppy food.

Evening: 1½ cups of puppy food mixed with a little water.

3–5 months: 2 meals a day

Morning: 2–3 cups of dry puppy food mixed with a little water and any supplement recommended by your breeder.

Evening: 2–3 cups of dry puppy food.

5 months–1 year: 2 meals a day

Morning: 3 cups of adult dry dog food with a protein level of 24%–26%, and any supplement recommended by your breeder.

Evening: 3–4 cups of adult dry dog food mixed with water.

The water-to-dry-food ratio should be approximately ¼ cup of water per 2 cups of dry food. Remember to keep fresh water available at all times. Each puppy is different and the above guidelines may have to be adjusted to your particular dog. Don't allow your puppy to get fat.

find a suitable dog food on the market that will satisfy even the dog with the most sensitive digestive system.

• Don't feed your dog an all-meat diet. Although that might sound good, it's anything but well-rounded.

The Components of Good Canine Nutrition

There are eight basic components that make up a nutritionally balanced feeding program for your Newf: proteins, carbohydrates, fats, vitamins, minerals, water, owner knowledge, and owner consistency.

• **Proteins** provide your pet with the amino acids it will need for growth, healthy muscle and bone, a well-functioning immune system, and production of enzymes and hormones and infection-fighting antibodies. Good sources of proteins are:

1. meat and poultry products;
2. milk products;
3. fish meal, corn, and soybeans.

• **Carbohydrates,** like proteins, will give your Newf the energy it needs to get through the day. Good sources of carbohydrates are:

1. cooked grain products;
2. vegetable matter;
3. processed starches.

• **Fats** provide a source of concentrated energy to your dog's system. Vitamins A, D, E, and K are fat-soluble vitamins and will help your Newf develop healthy skin, coat, and nervous system.

• **Vitamins** are necessary for general body functions. If you are feeding your dog a nutritionally complete food, added vitamin supplements are not necessary and may even have adverse effects. A good source of vitamins is a well-balanced, nutritionally complete dog food.

• **Minerals** are needed for normal body functions. Calcium and phosphorus help in the development and maintenance of strong bones, muscles, and teeth. Iron promotes healthy blood. A good source of minerals is a well-balanced, nutritionally complete dog food. Additional supplementation is not necessary and could have adverse effects.

• Don't arbitrarily feed additional vitamins or minerals without first consulting your veterinarian. Remember one of the cardinal rules of feeding: more is not better.

• **Water** is one of the most important components of your Newf's diet. Keep fresh water available at all times; don't allow it to become dirty or stale.

• Before you bring your Newf home, its breeder or former owner should acquaint you with its feeding regimen. If the breeder doesn't volunteer the information, ask for it. It's important to know what the dog was being fed and how often. Even if you do decide to change the feed, it should never be done abruptly, but gradually over a week or two.

Owner Knowledge

Your Newf's nutrition is in your hands. A giant breed like the Newf grows more rapidly than smaller breeds and has different nutritional needs. Your knowledge about those needs and what to feed your Newf can be a determining factor in its development.

Owner Consistency

One of the keys to your Newf's good health will be a good, consistent diet. Variety is not the spice of life when it comes to feeding your pet. Your Newf will thrive best on the same nutritionally balanced pet food, fed at regular intervals for most of its life.

Feeding the Newfoundland Puppy

Giant pup equals giant meals, right? Wrong! In fact, one of the biggest mistakes puppy owners make, regardless of the breed, is over-feeding their new baby. A fat, pudgy Newf pup does not a healthy Newf adult make. Why? Think about it in human terms. We've all read stories about how obese people are at a greater risk for serious health problems than their slender counterparts. It's exactly the same in the canine world. A fat dog has no

A puppy needs three meals a day between the ages of three and eighteen months, when its growth is the most rapid.

stamina. It's lazy. It doesn't move around much. The fatter it gets, the worse its situation becomes. Soon its breathing is affected; then its heart and other organs begin to fail. In a growing puppy, any extra weight is especially dangerous. The added pounds put extra pressure on its skeletal structure, thereby causing improper development of its bones and joints.

A healthy puppy is a lean puppy—but don't go to the opposite extreme. It shouldn't look emaciated either! To ascertain if your Newf puppy is in good weight, put your palms against its ribs. They should not poke out, but by exerting just the slightest pressure, you should clearly be able to feel each rib. Puppies gain and drop weight very quickly, so you'll have to be vigilant about your Newf's diet. Weigh it each week and keep a record. It should gain weight at a slow and steady rate as the rest of its body grows.

The amount to feed your Newf puppy is based on its nutritional needs at a specific time in its life. However, while the adult Newf is a comparatively small eater for its size, the Newf puppy is a heavy eater, especially between the ages of three and eighteen months, when its growth is the most rapid. During this period, the pup will eat several pounds of puppy food a day. The dog food you choose will have suggested daily amounts to feed the puppy on the back of the bag. But these are only suggested quantities that you may have to adjust for your particular pup. A young puppy of seven weeks, for example, needs three or four meals a day. Since its stomach is still small, it needs to eat more frequently.

Generally, it's wise to feed the pup three times a day: breakfast, lunch, and dinner. As it grows and begins to show no interest in lunch, it is telling you it's time to cut back on the amounts. Once you adjust the pup's new ration, you can divide it into two or three meals per day. Some breeders also suggest the "free choice" method of feeding, where food is put out once a day and the pup eats when it's hungry. There are several drawbacks to this method. If your Newf is housed in an outdoor kennel, food left out all day can attract insects and, in hot weather, unconsumed food invites

the growth of bacteria. A pup may also tend to gorge itself at one feeding, which could cause digestive problems.

Start your Newf on a kibbled puppy food that is generally between 26 and 31 percent protein. There is a difference of opinion among Newf breeders regarding the amount of protein needed in the growing pup's diet. Some breeders insist that diets high in protein cause muscles and tissue to develop more rapidly than bone and skeletal structure, causing extra stress to be put on the developing bones and skeleton, resulting in abnormalities. The quality is more important than the quantity of protein since, as already noted, the Newf puppy grows rapidly between the ages of three and eighteen months. Some breeders prefer their pups to be kept on puppy ration until one year old. However, if you begin to notice scabs on its rear and the dog doesn't have an allergy, suspect too much protein as the culprit and switch it to an adult dog food with between 21 and 25 percent protein. The condition should clear up in a few weeks. As we've already said, too many calories can be disastrous for the growing pup. But too much protein over a long period of time can also be very damaging to its general health. Although most bone and joint problems are thought to be genetic in origin, many are caused by improper diets. This is especially true in the giant breeds like the Newfoundland. By changing your pup to a lower protein food, you may be preventing orthopedic problems that could occur in later life.

Feeding the Adult Newfoundland

As your bouncing puppy approaches adulthood, you will notice that, along with its increase in size, it has had a marked decrease in activity level. Your Newf is no longer the tireless ball of fire who tears through the day at lightning speed, seeming never to become fatigued. It's normal for your Newf to settle down as it gets older. That doesn't mean it is or should become a couch potato by any means. It is just more selective about the times it wants to exercise and play. For this reason, an adult Newf does not need nearly as much food as its size would appear to dictate. That's why most nutritionists will warn you to be very wary of the feeding guidelines printed on the bag of dog food for a dog of your Newf's size. As it gets older, its metabolic rate decreases and thus cannot handle the huge quantities listed, so let your own common sense be the guide. And don't forget the "rib" test—if you can't feel them underneath all that coat, your Newf is too fat!

Feeding the Older Newfoundland

As your Newf approaches old age, its nutritional requirements will change again. When it reaches about seven or eight, you'll notice it starting to slow down a bit. It will have less energy and will need fewer calories, and less protein, carbohydrates, and fat than it did as a pup and an adult dog. At that point in its life, it's best to think of switching the dog to one of the "senior" dog food diets on the market. If you continue to feed it the same food and quantities that you did when it was younger, it will soon become overweight. It's especially important to keep the older Newf fit and trim in order to keep its heart and other vital organs functioning at optimum effectiveness. If you are unsure about what type of food to switch to or when, consult your veterinarian.

Types of Dog Food

Now that you have a fairly good handle on what constitutes a balanced diet for your Newf, the question arises

A dog biscuit makes an excellent treat to reward your Newf for a job well done.

as to which type of food to choose. There are three basic types of dog food commercially available: dry, moist, and semi-moist.

Dry Food. By far, the most popular food is a high-quality dry food. It's also the most economical. There are several other advantages to feeding a premium dry food. Not only is it nutritionally complete, supplying your Newf with all its caloric, vitamin, and mineral requirements, but it can be stored for months in an airtight container without refrigeration. Because of the crunchy substance of dry food, it's also better for your dog's teeth. It will help to keep its teeth and gums in good shape. Even though dry dog food may not look or smell particularly mouth-watering to you, it's extremely tasty to your dog. You will also find that when you choose a high-quality premium food, you will actually feed your dog much less than you would if it were on some of the other commercially prepared foods.

Moist Food. Moist foods come in cans. They are very tasty and most dogs will gobble them up in a flash. However, for a dog the size of a Newf, feeding an all-moist food is very expensive and there is no nutritional benefit. In fact, canned foods, which usually contain more salt and sugar derivatives than other type of food, can cause your Newf to put on unwanted pounds very quickly. What many owners choose to do instead is to mix a very small portion of moist with a basic dry food diet to make it more palatable.

Semi-Moist Food. The most eye-appealing dog foods are the semi-moist types that commonly come in burger, nugget, or chunk shapes that look exactly like real meat. Like dry food, semi-moist is fairly convenient and easy to feed. It's highly palatable, so most dogs like it without coaxing. Generally, it is more expensive to feed your Newf a semi-moist food. Remember too, that the soft consistency of the food will not give its teeth and gums the same benefits as a dry food will.

Homemade Diets

There is some debate about how nutritionally complete any commercial dog food is, given the processing that is involved. Some owners feel that the only way their pets will receive 100 percent sound and completely balanced food is if they make it themselves. Certainly, homemade diets are another alternative to feeding commercial foods, but if that's the route you choose to go, you'll need to follow strict nutritional guidelines. It's not enough to "set an extra place" at the table and simply give your Newf exactly what you eat. That's the best way to rob it of essential nutrients. So, unless you are well schooled in diet and nutrition, don't attempt to be your Newf's dietitian. If you are adamant

about feeding your Newf a homemade diet, however, ask your veterinarian to give you a recipe to follow. If your Newf has special dietary requirements because of allergies or other digestive problems, you may also want to consider the homemade diet alternative. However, there are specially prepared prescription diets available for just those problems. Remember, choosing to feed your dog a homemade diet will require diligence, added expense, and lots of added time.

Changing Foods

Once you have settled on a type and brand of dog food, stay with it unless your Newf has a bad reaction or your veterinarian recommends another feed. In order for your dog to get the most out of its diet, the diet must be consistent. Changes in your dog's food, when made at all, should be made slowly; otherwise, its stools could become loose and it may experience other digestive disorders. A good rule when changing to another feed is to do it over a week's time, gradually adding the new food to the ration of old food. This way, your Newf's digestive system won't be unduly stressed.

Water

Besides food, the most important component of your Newf's diet is water. Be sure it always has fresh water on hand, but don't allow it to gorge on water, especially after eating or exercise. Have a small amount always available and replenish it regularly. Water that is allowed to sit, especially outdoors, can become rife with bacteria, dirt, and insects.

Treats and Table Scraps

If you're like most dog owners, you won't be able to resist it when your Newf gives you that sad-eyed look while you're munching your lunchtime sandwich. Try anyway. Once you start feeding your Newf from the table, it's the beginning of the end. Throwing a 15-pound (7 kg) puppy a crust or two of your sandwich might seem cute, but several months down the line, when the 120-pound (54 kg) "Junior" bounds up for his share of your tuna on rye, it'll be a "horse of a different color." If you don't want your Newf to be a pest at your mealtimes, don't feed it from the table. If you want to give it some table scraps, do so in moderation, and then add them to its food at the appointed time.

Often you'll want to reward your Newf for a task well done. At that time, dog biscuits fit the bill nicely. Like commercial dog food, they are nutritionally balanced and can help to keep your Newf's teeth and gums clean. There are many varieties of dog treats on the market, but don't overdo it—treats can be very fattening. Use them judiciously. You may also want to give your Newf one of the many types of rawhide chews available in pet stores. For the most part, they sat-

isfy its need to chew and can prevent the pup from getting into trouble by chewing things like furniture instead. They can also keep your pup from getting bored when you're out of the house. However, some dogs have problems digesting the rawhide and if that's the case, discontinue giving them to your pet.

There are nonedible products on the market like nylon bones, which will also satisfy your pup's need to chew without incurring the risk of a possible digestive upset. However, be advised that other commercially available chew toys, like dried cow hooves, have been known to cause many a chipped tooth that can result in the need for extensive dental work. A good alternative for the young pup that will cause no damage and satisfy its chewing need is to take a rag or small towel, wet it down completely, knot it at each end and stick it in the freezer. In 15 minutes your pup will have a treat it can have fun with for hours with no dangerous repercussions!

As your Newf gets older, its metabolic rate decreases. To keep it in good condition, don't overfeed.

Grooming Your Newfoundland

When you first contemplated buying your Newf, you already knew that daily grooming would become a part of both your lives. Despite the Newfoundland's ample double coat, it's not hard to keep it looking its best. You should get your pup accustomed to being groomed as soon as you bring it home. Don't attempt anything too ambitious at first—a few seconds of brushing at a time, just to get it used to the idea, will suffice. It's doubly important to start grooming your Newf from puppyhood. Regular grooming not only makes it look terrific, but it will also help keep its skin and coat clean and healthy. Another reason to start your grooming sessions early on is purely practical: It's far easier to get a 20-pound (9 kg) Newf puppy accustomed to standing still for grooming than a 120-pound (54 kg) young adult!

To keep your Newfoundland looking good, you will need some basic grooming tools.

Start its grooming early. Your sacroiliac will thank you!

The amount of coat your Newf carries will depend on its bloodlines. Some dogs carry heavier coats than others. That's another reason it's always preferable to see the parents before purchasing a pup. The Newfoundland has a somewhat oily double coat—a top coat and an undercoat—which keeps it from getting wet to the skin when it's in the water. Generally, Newfs that are kept in outdoor kennels have more undercoat than a Newf that lives primarily in the house. Your Newf will shed more in the spring and fall, but daily brushing will keep it looking good all year round.

Remember, keep grooming sessions short at first, gradually increasing the time spent. Your Newf won't need serious grooming until it's about six months old. If you've made its early grooming sessions fun, when it's ready for the big time, it will not only be an old pro, but it'll look forward to its daily grooming. This will become part of the quality time you and your Newf spend together, exclusively.

Grooming Equipment

To groom your Newf, you'll need a place to do it and some basic tools.

The Grooming Table

The first investment you may want to make is in a grooming table. While it isn't necessary to groom your Newf on a table, it is easier for the groomer to stand while doing the job. For that reason, having a table on which the dog can either stand or lie is helpful. Extra-large grooming tables are available through pet supply stores for giant breeds like the Newf. It's a good idea to get your Newf used to being groomed in one particular spot, so you're not chasing it all around the house or yard with a pair of shears. Getting it accustomed to standing still on a grooming table will make the job easier for you and more pleasurable for the dog. The best way to get your puppy acclimated is to put it up on the table every day. Have a toy on hand and engage in a few seconds of play. Then give your pup a short brushing session. Increase your Newf's time on the table little by little, mixing play time with grooming. Then, when you're ready to do serious grooming, your Newf will climb up on the table willingly.

The grooming table should be very sturdy with a 24-inch (61 cm) wide top and a length of at least 36 inches (91 cm). The tabletop should also have rubber matting to keep your Newf's feet from slipping. The height of most tables is approximately 30 inches (76 cm), but you can also buy an adjustable one. Be sure to purchase an "arm" with your table. This device, which looks like an inverted letter "L," is screwed into the corner of the table and is adjustable to the height of your dog. At the end, there is a noose that you slip over your Newf's neck during the grooming session. This will help you keep your dog standing still and in one position while you groom. Never leave a dog unattended on a grooming table with its head in a noose—if your Newf were to jump off the table, it could injure itself. Such an experience would also make the dog loathe to ever want to get on a grooming table again.

Regular brushing will keep your Newf looking neat and clean.

Other Equipment

There are literally hundreds of grooming tools on the market. When you go to your favorite pet store, or look at a wholesale dog catalog, don't go crazy—you really only need six basic tools to get the job done.

One of the most important tools you'll use is a *slicker brush*. This is the best tool to use to get your puppy accustomed to grooming because it feels so wonderful on its body. The slicker brush is also invaluable for removing loose hair and any debris from its coat.

When grooming your Newf for show, a thinning shears will come in handy to shape the hair behind its ears.

Frequent combing and brushing will keep your Newf's coat looking neat and in good condition all year-round.

Once its adult coat starts to come in, you'll also need a *coarse-toothed comb* to get down deep to its skin and a *rake* for getting rid of all that excess dead hair.

Another essential item is the *toenail clipper*. Don't try to use human toenail clippers on your Newf. Choose one designed for big dogs. Make sure the model has replacement blades available since tough Newf nails wear out blades rather quickly. Most owners shy away from clipping nails, but once you accustom your Newf to the procedure it's very simple and painless.

You'll also need *thinning shears*. It's wise to invest in a good pair with fine teeth, as these will give your Newf the best, most professional look.

A pair of *blunt-edged shears* is also very handy, especially when you want to strip all the hair that collects between your Newf's toes.

Grooming Your Newfoundland Puppy

Your Newf puppy will not require a great deal of grooming, but it's a good idea to get it used to being groomed at a young age so you won't have problems keeping your pet looking good once it's older and needs more elaborate grooming.

• Lift your pup onto its grooming table. Let it sit or lie down. Remember, make it fun. Be touchy and playful with the pup as it rolls around on the table, then get down to the business at hand.

• First, tackle the toenails. Hold the toenail clippers and starting gently, pull one leg toward you. Make sure you have a firm grip and clip only the hooked part of the nail. If you cut more, you run the risk of cutting into the *quick*, which contains the nerve and vessels. If cut, it will cause bleeding from the vein. If that happens, have a styptic pencil or coagulant powder on hand. In puppies with white toenails, you can see the quick as a pinkish area. In dogs with black nails, make sliver-like cuts until you see a blackish, moist looking center. That's the quick. Don't go any further.

• Next, proceed to brush your Newf for a few seconds. If it starts to get impatient, don't let it jump off the table, as injury can result. Instead, settle it down and then lift it from the table.

Bathing

• At some point, you'll want to give your dog its first bath. Since Newfs love water, this should be fairly easy, but introduce it gently. While it's a pup, you can easily pick it up and put it into your bathtub.

• Start with only a few inches of water and throw in some of its toys. Get it used to splashing around and having fun in the tub. When it's ready for its first real bath, it'll already have a familiarity with the tub and will accept being there.

• Wet it down with a sponge, while praising it for its good behavior. Spray attachments are also good and tend to get the job done more quickly and with less mess. The spray may frighten the pup at first, but if you acclimate it gently, it soon will think that's all part of the fun at hand.

• Use either a commercial baby shampoo or one of the special dog shampoos on the market.

• Don't use an insecticide product unless the pup has fleas or ticks (see page 80). Be sure not to get the shampoo in its eyes or ears.

• Once you've soaped the pup down, use either the spray attachment or a bucket with clean water and a sponge to rinse it. You can also pour water gently over the pup until it is rinsed. Don't leave any shampoo on its coat.

• After your Newf is completely rinsed, have a big, bulky towel ready and begin to dry it. Most dogs love the sensation of being dried with a towel. If you have a dog blow dryer, use that. Once your Newf gets used to the sound, it'll love it. Don't use your human hair dryer, however, unless it has a "No Heat" setting. The heat setting on human hair dryers is much too hot for your puppy.

Unless you show your Newf or it gets into a lot of grime and dirt outside, you probably won't have to bathe it more than every few months—or longer, depending on how clean you keep its coat with brushings and combings in between.

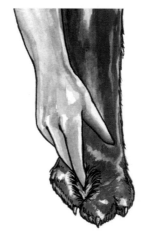

When grooming the adult Newf, you will need to use a thinning shears to remove the hair between its toes.

Grooming Your Adult Newfoundland

As your Newf gets older, your grooming sessions will get longer and more ambitious. Your main objective is to keep the dog looking neat and clean at all times and free of mats, which can cause skin problems. Regular combing and brushing, along with infrequent baths will accomplish that. However, there are also a few other areas to which you'll want to attend to. Besides clipping its toenails and brushing its coat, you'll also need to remove the excess hair between its toes and keep the area around its ears and neck shaped with the thinning shears and

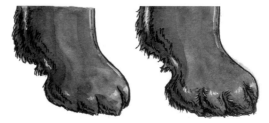

Left: Groomed toes and nails
Right: Toes and nails before grooming.

Clean your Newf's ears regularly by moistening a ball of cotton with an ear cleaner or a mixture of hydrogen peroxide and alcohol.

the blunt scissors. If the hair at its hock is very long or straggly, make it neater by holding a straight scissors pointing down and then trimming the hair around the hock to no more than one inch (2.5 cm) long. Trim its ears by cutting around the ear, especially the hair behind the fold. To make the look more professional, blend the edges with the thinning sheers.

Proper Care of Nails, Ears, and Eyes

Nails. We've already discussed how to trim your Newf's nails. But it's also necessary to stress the importance of keeping them cut. And don't forget the dewclaws (vestiginal toes). Leaving them uncut can cause the nail to curve back and grow into the skin of the leg. Also remember to file your

Newf's nails after trimming. If you leave jagged edges, your dog can hurt itself if it scratches a part of its body. It will also give you a nasty scratch if it playfully hits you with its paw. You can use any heavy-duty nail file to get the job done.

Ears. Always keep your Newf's ears clean. There are many commercial ear washes on the market that will do the job, or you can make your own. Routinely dampen a ball of cotton with hydrogen peroxide and alcohol and gently clean the inside of the dog's ear. Use another ball of cotton to dry the ear. If you use a commercial drying powder, be sure the ear is completely dry before dusting it. Administering powder to a moist ear can cause the powder to cake and obstruct the air flow, which can precipitate waxing or scratching. Never use a swab or Q-Tip to clean or probe inside your Newf's ear; you could cause damage. With regular care, your Newf's ears should remain clean, healthy, and odor-free.

Eyes. Since your Newf will probably spend a great deal of time outdoors, its eyes are particularly prone to injury and/or infection. Keep a careful watch on its eyes and, should they appear red or watery, you can treat them with a mild eyewash that is commercially available over the counter at drugstores. A baby eyewash is recommended. If the condition worsens, consult your veterinarian.

Showing Your Newfoundland

Before buying your Newfoundland, one of the things you will have to decide is whether to pick a "show-quality" or a "pet-quality" puppy/dog. If you want to show your dog in conformation, you must pick a Newf that most closely typifies the standard for the breed. As a working breed, the Newfoundland is particularly well-suited to performing tasks of any kind, and for that reason it is a natural in the show ring. Unlike obedience or water trials that require specific skills, the only mandate for competing in conformation is that your dog look good and move well in the ring. Simply put, it's a beauty contest. But, like any activity you and your Newf do together, showing is fun and rewarding, and if you have a good dog, it can lead to a championship.

Before showing your Newf, first have it evaluated by several people who are knowledgeable about the breed. Even though you may have bought a show puppy at nine weeks, by the time it's six months (the earliest you can enter it in conformation), it may not be the perfect specimen you expected. While breeders try to determine with reasonable accuracy which puppies will be show-quality, often the difference between a show and a pet pup is so slight that it may not become apparent until the puppy starts to mature. Another reason to have your puppy evaluated before showing it is to learn its faults. No dog is perfect and a professional with a good eye will be able to guide you on the best way to minimize its faults and accentuate its better features.

The next step is to attend several dog shows and learn ring procedures. You can handle your own dog in the ring or hire a professional handler. Many people who have shown their own dogs to a championship will tell you that there is nothing more exciting than going in the ring and winning those points together. Most dog clubs offer regular conformation classes for owners who wish to compete with their dogs. In the United States, in order to become a champion of record, your dog must win 15 points. Two sets must be major points (three-, four-, or five-point blocks) and must be won under two different judges.

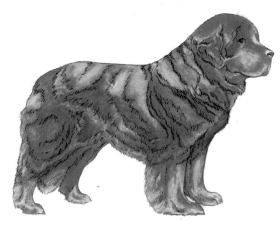

An adult Newf dog stands 28 inches high at the shoulder and weighs approximately 130 pounds.

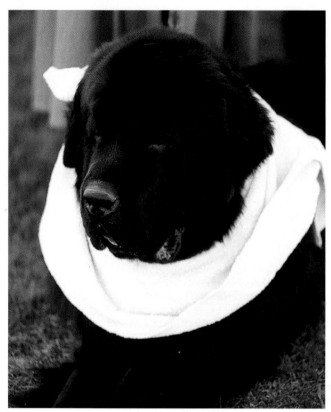

Showing your Newfoundland in conformation requires that he look good and move well in the ring.

deep-bodied with heavy bones and powerful musculature. Standing over 26 inches at the shoulder, its weight reaches about 150 pounds.

Size. Large, massive size is desirable in both the male and the bitch, but never at the expense of balance, structure, and proper gait. The average adult male stands 28 inches (71 cm) high at the shoulder; adult bitches, 24 inches (61 cm) high. A full-grown male can weigh between 130 and 150 pounds (59–68 kg); a full-grown bitch, 100 and 120 pounds (45–54 kg). The Newfoundland is slightly longer than it is tall from the point of the shoulder to the point of the buttocks and from the withers to the ground. It has considerable substance, which is determined by the spring of its rib, strong muscles, and heavy bones.

Head. The Newfoundland has a massive head with a broad skull, slightly arched crown, and strongly developed occipital bone. Its cheeks are well-developed. The eyes are dark brown (browns and grays may have lighter eyes), relatively small, deep-set, and spaced wide apart. The eyelids fit closely with no inversion. The ears are relatively small and triangular with rounded tips. They are set on the skull, level with or slightly above the brow, and lie close to the head. When the ear is brought forward, it reaches to the inner corner of the eye on the same side. The expression is soft and reflects the characteristics of the breed: benevolence, intelligence, and dignity.

The forehead and face are smooth and free of wrinkles. The slope of the stop is moderate, the muzzle clean-cut, broad throughout its length, and deep. Depth and length are approximately equal. The top of the muzzle is rounded. The bridge, in profile, is straight or only slightly arched. Teeth meet in a level or scissor bite.

Neck, Topline, Body. The neck is strong and well-set on the shoulders

As a breed, Newfoundlands have fared quite well in the show ring. In 1984, Am. Can. Ch. Seaward's Blackbeard, ROM, the most winning Newfoundland in the history of the breed, became the first Newf ever to win Best in Show at the most prestigious dog show of them all—the Westminster Kennel Club.

The American Kennel Club Standard for the Newfoundland

Appearance

The Newfoundland is a large, heavily coated dog. It is well-balanced and

and long enough for proud head carriage. The back is strong, broad, and muscular, and is level from just behind the withers to the croup (rump). The chest is full and deep with the brisket (breast or lower chest) reaching at least down to the elbows. Ribs are well-sprung, with the anterior third of the rib cage tapered to allow clearance. The flank is deep. The croup is broad and slopes slightly. The tail set follows the natural line of the croup. The tail is broad at the base and strong. It has no kinks and the distal bone reaches the hock. When the dog is standing relaxed, its tail hangs straight or with a slight curve at the end. When the dog is in motion, the tail is carried out, but it does not curl over the back.

Forequarters. The shoulders are muscular and well laid back. Elbows lie directly below the highest point of the withers. Forelegs are muscular, heavily boned, straight, and parallel to each other. The elbows point directly to the rear. The distance from the elbow to the ground equals about half the dog's height. Pasterns are strong and slightly sloping. The feet are proportionate to the body size, webbed and cat-foot in type. Dewclaws may be removed.

Hindquarters. The rear assembly is powerful, muscular, and heavily boned. Viewed from the rear, the legs are straight and parallel. Viewed from the side, the thighs are broad and fairly long. Stifles and hocks are well bent and the line from hock to ground is perpendicular. Hocks are well let down. Hind feet are similar to the front feet. Dewclaws should be removed.

Coat. The adult Newfoundland has a flat, water-resistant double coat that tends to fall back into place when rubbed against the nap. The outer coat is coarse, moderately long, and full, either straight or with a wave. The undercoat is soft and dense,

One of the unique features of the Newf's double coat is that it is water resistant.

The Newf's great strength and power is derived from its massive musculature.

although it is often less dense during the summer months or in warmer climates. Hair on the face and muzzle is short and fine. The backs of the legs are feathered all the way down. The tail is covered with long, dense hair. Excess hair may be trimmed for neatness. Whiskers need not be trimmed.

Color. Color is secondary to type, structure, and soundness. Recognized Newfoundland colors are black, brown, gray, and white and black.

• Solids—blacks, browns, and grays—may appear as solid colors or solid colors with white at any, some, or all of the following locations: chin, chest, toes, and tip of tail. Any amount of white found at these locations is typical and is not penalized. Also typical are a tinge of bronze on a black or a gray coat and lighter furnishings on a brown or a gray coat.

• Landseer—a white base coat with black markings. Typically, the head is solid black, or black with white on the muzzle, with or without a blaze. There is a separate black saddle and black on the rump extending onto a white tail.

Markings on either solid colors or Landseers might deviate considerably from those described above and should be penalized only to the extent of the deviation. Clear white or white with minimal ticking is preferred.

Beauty of markings should be considered only when comparing dogs of otherwise comparable quality and never at the expense of type, structure, and soundness.

Any colors or combinations of color not specifically described are disqualified.

Gait. The Newfoundland in motion has good reach and strong drive; it gives the impression of effortless power. Its gait is smooth and rhythmic, covering the maximum amount of ground with the minimum number of steps. Forelegs and hindlegs travel straight forward. As the dog's speed increases, the legs tend

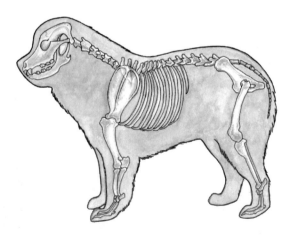

A sound Newfoundland will have a perfect skeletal structure to ensure stamina and correct movement.

toward single tracking. When moving, a slight roll of the skin is characteristic of the breed. Essential to good movement is the balance of correct front and rear assemblies.

Temperament

Sweetness of temperament is the hallmark of the Newfoundland. This is the single most important characteristic of the breed. A multipurpose dog, at work it is tireless and eager to please and at home it is a fun-loving and devoted companion. It is equally at home on land or in water and possesses natural life-saving abilities.

If you show your Newf, you will have to learn how to "stack" or set up its front and rear for judging: Left: too wide; Center: correct; Right: too close.

Grooming for Show

If you plan to show your Newf in conformation classes, you must groom it according to the standard for the breed. Remember, showing is like a beauty contest, nothing more, nothing less. In order to make your Newf stand out and be competitive in the conformation ring, you must accentuate its positive features and downplay the negative. Your Newf must look balanced and in proportion and very often the difference between a show winner and loser is a matter of good grooming. Let a professional handler/breeder teach you how to groom your Newf for show. They will have the most practiced eye to evaluate your dog's best features and groom it accordingly. There are also grooming videos on the market, available through pet catalogs, which will give you step-by-step instructions for grooming your breed.

When grooming your Newf for show, always use a thinning shears. Cut the hair in the direction of its natural lie only. Avoid removing too much hair, since, as you get down to the skin, the color of the hair usually becomes lighter and you want to avoid a patchy look. If your Newf has an excessive amount of hair on its throat,

neck, and shoulders, you should use your thinning shears to shorten it and thus give your Newf a longer neckline. To make your Newf's neck look longer and more stately, draw an imaginary line from the back of its ear to the middle of its shoulder. Trim below the line, around to the front of the neck to the other side. Be careful not to trim any hair above the line. Other areas you might need to work on are your Newf's shoulder and elbow. Excessive hair here will make its legs look short and squat. To correct this, thin the hair above the elbow. The effect will be to make its elbow look higher and, consequently, its leg will look longer.

Once you have your Newf's front stacked, work on its rear: Left: cow-hocked; Center: correct; Right: too close (toeing-in).

During a conformation show, the judge will approach your Newf and go over it to assess how closely it matches the AKC established standard for the breed.

Even a Newf that isn't show quality can look like a star with proper grooming.

If your Newf's shoulders are too steep, you'll need to thin the hair there as well so it will appear to be well laid back. A good way to check if your Newf's shoulders have the right lay-back is to put one hand on the withers and the other on the point of the shoulder. If the line between the two appears steep, you'll need to thin the hair to make it less apparent.

Sometimes a Newf will have too much hair on the back of its buttocks, making it look out of balance and longer than it is. To correct this, use the thinning sheers, angling the point downward, and go deeply into the coat. When using the thinning shears, always follow up with combing to remove the excess hair.

Of course, if your Newf isn't show-quality, all the grooming tricks in the world won't make it a winner, but if you have a good dog, expert grooming can make it really shine.

A dog competing in the conformation ring must not only look good, but also exhibit the sweet temperament that is the hallmark of the breed.

When not competing, the Newf is a great big clown that loves to let its hair down and have fun with its master.

Raising Quality Newfoundlands

Should You Breed Your Newfoundland?

Your beautiful Newfoundland is the love of your life. Consequently, you may ask yourself when you should breed it. Stop right there. The question isn't *when* you should breed, but should you breed *at all*. Taking steps to bring life into the world, canine or human, requires a great deal of soul-searching and above all, a deep understanding of the responsibilities entailed. Just because you buy a great Newf, it doesn't follow that you should start your own breeding program. Breeding quality dogs is hard work. It is not and should never be done for monetary profit.

Experienced and reputable breeders will tell you that they barely break even financially on litters they produce. Why do they do it? To perfect the breed and assure its survival in the best, most true-to-standard form. Problems in the breed as a whole develop and are passed along to future generations when breeding is done indiscriminately by people with little or no expertise. The only real control is good, sound breeding programs left in the hands of well-informed, experienced, conscientious, and careful people.

If you are so crazy about your Newf and can't wait to get another, go back to your breeder and buy one. Don't impulsively decide to raise Newfs yourself. Think about it from a purely practical standpoint. One Newf, great. Two, even better. But what about a litter of

ten? In six months they will be big, strapping, young dogs. What if you can't sell them all? What will you do? Panic? Reduce your price and practically give them away to anyone just to get them out of the house? Therein lies the problem with uninformed and inexperienced breeders. The real victims of your vanity are the puppies you allowed to come into the world.

As you know, before you decided on a Newf yourself, you had to consider many things. First and foremost, you had to ask if your lifestyle could support a dog with the size and requirements of a Newf. There are not many potential dog owners who could have answered "yes" to that one. That alone should discourage the potential breeder. Consider the staggering number of dogs, both purebred and mixed, that are put to death each year because they were unwanted. Don't allow an animal that has passed through your care to become one of those tragic statistics if you can help it. One way to make a difference is to be realistic and honest before deciding to breed your dog.

There are other considerations as well. You may indeed have a lovely Newf, but that doesn't mean it is good breeding stock. Usually the breeder will keep the best dogs. Out of a litter of ten, maybe one or two will be breeding stock. If you bought a pet-quality dog, under no circumstances should it be bred. The reason the dog was sold as a pet rather than for show is because it had some undesirable characteristic that should not be passed on.

Another thing—don't believe all the old wives' tales. A bitch does not have to be bred to live a full, contented life. Nor does a male need to be mated in order to insure a good temperament. That's nothing more than backyard crockery. There is no scientific evidence that bred dogs live longer or healthier lives than their unbred counterparts. On the other hand, there is substantial scientific data available to support the contention that spayed/neutered dogs do enjoy longer, healthier lives. Furthermore, if you are not showing your dog, or if your dog is pet-quality, it should be neutered. Only animals used for breeding purposes should remain intact.

Having said all of the above, if you are set on becoming a student of the breed and are willing to put in all the time, dedication, and money it will take to raise good Newfoundlands, then breeding may be something to consider. There is nothing like the feeling of knowing that you have helped to produce a litter of fine, healthy puppies that will not only go on to enrich the lives of other special people like yourself, but also enrich the breed as well. Added to that are the abiding human friendships you will make through your contact with other breeders and owners.

Types of Breeding

In your study of dog breeding you will learn that there are several types of breeding.

Inbreeding means the breeding of very closely related dogs—father to daughter, mother to son. It's an easy way to replicate desirable characteristics, but not necessarily a good one unless done sparingly and by extremely experienced breeders.

Linebreeding is the more common type of breeding used in most ken-

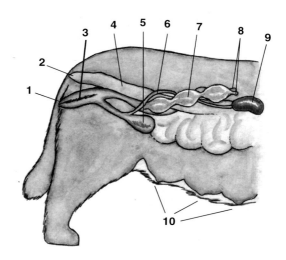

The internal organs of the female: 1. vulva 2. anus 3. vagina 4. rectum 5. bladder 6. ureter 7. developing embryo 8. ovaries 9. kidney 10. mammary glands

nels. It is the mating of relatives several times removed—a half-granddaughter to a half-grandfather, cousin to cousin, nephew to aunt. Although it may take the breeder several generations to produce the precise results desired, linebreeding is the safest way to get the characteristics the breeder is looking for.

Outcrossing is another type of breeding, in which a breeder mates two unrelated dogs. Most breeders outcross every few generations in order to keep their lines fresh. However, continual outcrossing will result in a confused pedigree and make it impossible for the breeder to predict either type or characteristics from the breeding.

It's important to understand that neither inbreeding nor linebreeding can create genes that were not already present. Both methods simply bring the desired and undesired dominant and recessive characteristics to the forefront. But, just as inbreeding and

67

No matter how much you love your Newfoundland, you must be realistic and do a lot of soul-searching before deciding to breed it.

season, or at about two years old. At that point, don't delay because many bitches will never conceive if they are much over the desired age at the time of their first mating.

Usually, heat periods will occur twice a year, six months apart and last for 21 days each. Your Newf is only capable of conceiving during this time. The first 10 days of the bitch's season is called *proestrus*. On her first day of heat, you'll notice a thin red discharge, which fades as the season progresses.

Estrus is the second phase of the bitch's season. This occurs at about the tenth day after the first red discharge was observed in proestrus. During this stage, which usually lasts about seven days, a thin clear discharge is visible. At this point her vulva, which is the exterior portion of the bitch's reproductive tract, will begin to swell. Somewhere between day 10 and day 18 (counting from the first day of proestrus), ovulation and conception occur. Even though the male will be attracted to the female throughout her heat period, it is only at this time that the bitch will allow him to mount and breed her.

If a mating has been accomplished, your bitch's body will begin to prepare for the coming birth. The vulva will remain swollen and the bitch will enter *metestrus*. During this stage, the mammary glands ready themselves to produce milk. At approximately the twenty-eighth to the thirty-fifth day after breeding, you should have your veterinarian palpate your Newf to see if she is in whelp (pregnant).

linebreeding bring recessive and dominant traits to the surface, so too does outcrossing. When outcrossing, it is imperative that the pedigrees on both sides be scrupulously checked so undesirable characteristics do not result.

The Estrous Cycle

Unlike most breeds, the Newfoundland female is slow to mature. Your female probably won't come into her first season or heat period, also known as *estrus* until she's about 14 to 18 months old. It could happen sooner, however, so be prepared. You should not breed your bitch until she comes into her second

Selecting a Stud Dog

Once you have carefully examined the pros and cons of breeding and have decided to breed your female, the next logical step is to find the right male. The objective is to match the bitch with a stud dog that will enhance the female's strong points and not exhibit any of the faults. When you consider a stud dog, ask to see medical records certifying that the dog is in good health and free of congenital defects like hip dysplasia (see page 85) and any heart abnormalities. Another important consideration is the temperament of the stud dog. Do not breed your bitch to a dog with aggressive tendencies.

One of the common mistakes first-time breeders often make is choosing a stud dog because he is doing a lot of winning in the conformation ring. Remember the old adage, looks can be deceiving? Nowhere is this more applicable than in the breeding of purebred dogs. There are many tricks to making an average dog look like a champion in the conformation ring. Furthermore, a dog can look great, win lots of ribbons, and still have congenital defects that are not visually apparent. After reviewing the dog's health records and X rays, ask to see a pedigree and also ask for the names and phone numbers of people who have puppies sired by the dog. A few phone calls will give you a good overview of the quality of the litters he has sired. If the owner of the stud dog won't cooperate, eliminate the dog from consideration as a stud for your bitch.

The female Newfoundland is an attentive mother and doesn't like to be away from her pups for long periods during their first few weeks of life.

A Contract

Obviously, choosing a stud dog will require a lot of preparation and research on your part. So plan well in advance. Don't wait until your bitch comes into season. One way to find the right stud dog is to talk to other breeders and evaluate the progeny of their stud dogs. Your objective is to choose a stud that will complement your bitch's strong points. Don't choose a dog that shares her faults. Once you have selected a stud dog, draw up a contract with the owner. Usually a stud fee is agreed upon and/or a provision that the stud's owner can have the pick of one or more of the puppies. Your contract should also contain a guarantee that your bitch will come into whelp and bear puppies. If the mating does not take, you should have the option of the service of the stud dog when your bitch comes into season again. You may also request the return of the stud fee.

Mating

Before the proposed mating takes place, you should have your bitch checked to make sure she is in

69

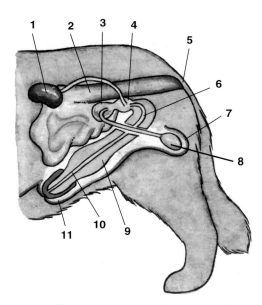

The internal organs of the male: 1. kidney 2. rectum 3. bladder 4. prostate 5. anus 6. urethra 7. scrotum 8. testes 9. bulb 10. penis 11. sheath.

excellent health and free from worms. All vaccinations should be up-to-date. Due to their size and heavy coats, Newfoundlands will sometimes need assistance during the mating. A bitch may even sit or lie down while the male is trying to breed her. It's best to enlist the help of a breeder friend the first time you attempt to breed your bitch. The bitch should also be bred every other day until the male is refused, just to be sure the mating has taken place. Don't ever allow your bitch to run loose while in season. Any other male on the loose can also breed it. Don't even allow the bitch to remain with the stud dog alone. Breeding should always be supervised. Be aware that your bitch could mate with another dog other than the stud at this time. If that happens, the parentage of the puppies will be in question. During her week of estrus, keep your bitch away from all unneutered males, except the stud dog.

Pregnancy

The average length of gestation for a Newf is nine weeks, approximately 59 to 63 days. One of the first signs that your bitch has conceived is a change in personality. Often she will become more loving and want to be near you more than usual. Her appetite will also change. Most Newf bitches in whelp have increased appetites. Occasionally, a pregnant bitch will refuse to eat during the first week and may even exhibit traditional signs of "morning sickness." If the condition continues longer, take your female to the veterinarian because a more serious problem may be present. Pyometra, or pus in the uterus, is a potentially fatal condition that can develop following estrus, especially at the four- to six-week mark. If the bitch's abdomen appears distended, if she appears depressed and some-what disoriented, if her water con-sumption increases and she refuses food and begins to vomit, get her to the veterinarian immediately.

By about the fourth or fifth week after the mating, you should begin to increase her food, as your female will start to require more nourishment. It's a good idea to feed her several small meals a day rather than two large ones—but don't allow overindulgence. As in human pregnancies, your Newf shouldn't be allowed to put on too much extra weight. Exercise is also important during pregnancy. Even though the bitch's activity level may taper off, moderate exercise is neces-sary to maintain muscle tone and gen-eral good health in preparation for the coming whelping. If your Newf bitch is one of those active types that nothing slows down, even the upcoming whelp-ing, you may just have to restrict her activity yourself at about the fifth week.

As the birth time draws nearer, it's a good idea to separate the bitch from any other dogs in the household. Any rough play should be avoided.

False Pregnancy

Occasionally, a bitch will exhibit all the symptoms of being pregnant even though she has not conceived. Her body may produce milk and she may exhibit other physical and physiological signs of pregnancy. However, other underlying problems like ovarian cysts and pyometritis, could be the cause. These conditions are more prevalent in bitches that have never had puppies. In any case, don't just dismiss false pregnancy as a hormonal imbalance that will eventually pass. Let your veterinarian check your bitch at the three-week mark to be sure she is pregnant.

Pre-Whelping Preparations

Don't wait until the last minute to prepare for the birth of puppies. It's imperative that you have everything ready in advance, just in case your Newf goes into labor earlier than expected. Decide where you want her to give birth and then construct a whelping box. Choose a part of the house that is warm and quiet. It's best to locate the whelping box in an area with easy access to the yard and the laundry room. If this is your first time as a dog midwife, you may want to have a breeder friend on call or see if your veterinarian will be available to help with the birth.

Be sure to have all the necessary supplies on hand well in advance. These supplies include:
• a heating pad
• lots of newspapers
• surgical silk or dental floss to tie around the puppies' umbilical cords after they are cut
• a scissors and hemostatic forceps to cut and clamp the umbilical cord

• a thermometer to take the bitch's temperature before and after whelping
• hand towels to dry the puppies and larger towels to put under the bitch during and after the whelping because your bitch will have quite a bit of discharge both during whelping and in the ten days following
• a scale to weigh each puppy after delivery and in the days following

You should keep a chart of each puppy's weight so you can tell which one is gaining or losing weight. You may also want to have knitting yarn in various colors available to identify each puppy. Tie it snugly around the puppy's neck, not too tight, but not loose enough for it to get its foot caught in it. Puppies do a lot of rolling around, so this can happen easier than you may think. Be vigilant. Also be sure to change the yarn every day as the puppies will grow very fast. A less risky manner of identification is to paint a different color nail polish on the back toenail of each puppy.

The Whelping Box

You can construct your own whelping box from plywood or purchase one. For a dog the size of a Newf, the box should be at least 4 feet (1.2 m) by 6 feet (2 m) so the bitch is able to lie comfortably on her side. It should be at least 18 to 24 inches (46–61 cm) high and have an opening or door that the bitch can get into and out of easily. If you intend to keep the newborn puppies in the whelping box for the first few weeks, a larger box will be necessary.

Once the box is completed, place it in an area of the room you have set aside that is warm and away from drafts and household traffic. Line the box with layers of new, unhandled newspapers. Do not use the colored sections as the print can be toxic. As the papers become soiled, replace them with fresh ones.

Your Newfoundland puppies will be ready to go out into the world and to their new homes by the age of twelve weeks. Under no circumstances should a pup be sold before eight weeks of age.

Make sure the box has a rail all around the inside wall about 5 inches (13 cm) above the floor. This is to keep the pups from inadvertently being crushed between the mother and the side of the box.

Whelping

Even though your Newf will probably be able to take charge of whelping her pups, it's wise to stay close at hand just in case you have to help out, especially if this is your female's first litter. It's also a good idea to check with your veterinarian and advise him or her as the time draws nearer for your bitch to whelp. Be sure you have a day and night number where you can contact the veterinarian should a problem arise.

Temperature

You'll know the time is at hand when your bitch begins to act anxious. The abdomen will drop several days before the delivery. Body temperature will also drop, so you should begin taking the bitch's temperature three times a day and recording it about a week before you expect the puppies to arrive. Normal temperature is between 100°F and 101°F (37.8 to 38°C). If it drops to between 98°F and 99.5°F (36.7 to 37.2°C) and remains there for several hours, you can be fairly certain that your female will deliver within the next 24 hours. It's best to confine her to the room with the whelping box. If she has to go out, take her on a leash and then return her to the room you've set aside.

The Amniotic Sac

Each puppy arrives in an amniotic sac. The bitch will begin to tear the sac open and lick the puppy dry, stimulating and cleaning it. Newf bitches are not always the best whelpers compared to other breeds. If your bitch does not tend to her newborn immediately, be prepared to step in and break the sac yourself with your finger. Pull it back from the puppy's nose and mouth. Then give the bitch another chance to take over, but if she does not, you'll have to do it for her. Use a hand towel to dry the pup and stimulate its breathing. Be sure its nostrils are free of any liquid.

The Umbilical Cord

An afterbirth and umbilical cord are expelled after each puppy. The mother will usually tear the cord and consume the afterbirth. Again, if the bitch does not sever the cord, take your forceps and clamp the cord about one inch (2.5 cm) from the pup; cut the cord between the forceps and placenta with the scissors. Then dab the end with alcohol or organic iodine. Tie a piece of dental floss around the base of the cord. Many times, the bitch will insist on eating all the placenta. Some breeders recommend not allowing her to consume more than two, as it could affect her appetite for regular food later on. However, others feel it is more prudent not to interfere with nature and let the bitch consume as many of the placentas as she chooses. Be sure to count all the placentas that have been expelled. It's important that the bitch doesn't retain any of them in her body, as infection could develop.

It will take anywhere from a few minutes to a few hours between the delivery of puppies. After each pup is born, replace the soiled papers and towels with fresh ones. Your bitch may also feel the need to go outside and relieve

Puppies coming through the birth canal in amniotic sacs.

herself between deliveries. A word of advice: If it's nighttime, take along a towel and a flashlight just in case the bitch drops one puppy on the walk.

If your bitch appears to be straining during the delivery without producing a puppy, the little one may be in the so-called "breech" position. Call your veterinarian immediately for assistance.

After each pup is delivered and cleaned, weigh it, affix its I.D. (whatever method of identification you've chosen), and return it to the whelping box so it

Puppy coming through birth canal in breech position.

can start to nurse immediately. Once all the puppies are delivered, your bitch will probably want a nice walk and then a long nap. Be sure the puppies are kept warm. Though many breeders use heating pads to keep newborns warm, this is not necessary and can harm the puppies. Newborns are frequently "roasted" by heating pads. If the puppies pile up and are dry, out of drafts, and at room temperature, no artificial heat is necessary to keep them warm. If you do use a heating pad, be sure it is set on the lowest temperature. Cover it with a towel and use a thermometer to keep the temperature consistent. Also, make sure an unheated area is accessible to the puppies.

During the first few days of the puppies' lives, you will have to keep a close watch on them. The bitch will want to stay close to them, but it's important to make sure the mother doesn't accidentally sit on one of the pups and smother it.

Care of the New Mother and Puppies

A few days after the delivery, ask your veterinarian to make a house call to check the mother and pups just to make sure everything is all right. Your Newf will be a wonderful mother and won't want to be away from the pups for any length of time. You can help out during the first few weeks by making sure fresh water is always available. Feed your bitch frequently, slowly enticing her back to eating all of her favorite foods. Add chopped beef, shredded chicken, chicken soup, or even canned dog food to her regular dry ration. Your female should begin to eat two good-sized meals each day. Ask your veterinarian about the appropriate feeding guidelines.

You will also have to be sure the puppies are getting enough to eat during the first few weeks. If the puppies are hungry or are not nursing enough,

they will let you know by whining and crying. You should also weigh the pups regularly to keep track of their weight gain. Any weight loss in one of the pups will alert you that there is a problem and you will need to consult your veterinarian.

Weaning the pups from sole dependence on their mother's milk to solid food should begin after the puppies' eyes open (at about two weeks). Introduce the pups to moistened bits of dry food and let them lick it from your fingers just to get the taste. At three weeks old, they can begin lapping puppy food that you have crushed and soaked with warm water from a flat-bottomed pan. Feed them only once a day until they get the idea. Gradually decrease the amount of water you mix with the food. Keep a separate water pan available. The pups are normally completely weaned between five and eight weeks old. By the time they are six to eight weeks old, they will be eating three meals a day. To avoid an unsightly mess around chow time, don't feed them in the whelping box.

When the pups are six weeks old, it is time to take them to the veterinarian for the first series of their puppy vaccinations. They will also be checked for worms, as newborns may contract parasites from their mother. By now, your little black bundles of joy are big enough to be getting into a heap of trouble at home, so be vigilant. Keep the pups confined to their puppy pens and be sure the house is puppy-proofed (see page 26). At this stage, your pups are beginning to learn their order in the pack. They will engage in play and will attempt to establish dominance. Mother Dog will correct any unwanted behavior. This is one reason it is extremely important to keep the pups with their mother and littermates until they are at least eight weeks old; otherwise, they may have difficulty getting along with other dogs as they grow older.

Socializing the Puppies

From the time the puppies are three weeks old, they should begin to socialize with humans. Give each pup individual attention every day so that it will get used to being touched and spoken to. When the puppies reach seven weeks of age, they will be ready to bond with their human companions. Do everything possible to build up their trust and self-confidence. During the crucial learning period from seven to twelve weeks, it's a good idea to keep the littermates apart some of the time. This will insure that no one will have the opportunity to become the leader of the pack and dominate the others. The pups should begin to look toward their human companion as their alpha leader.

When the pups reach the age of eight to twelve weeks, they will be ready to go off in the world to their new homes. Before sending them to their new families, they should have complete physical examinations, including having their hearts checked by the veterinarian for any abnormality, since Newfs can develop heart problems in puppyhood.

Finding a Home for Your Puppies

That brings us to the final stage in the whole breeding process—finding the right home for your Newf puppies. When you first decided to breed your bitch, finding good homes for the puppies was one of the paramount considerations. As stated earlier, it isn't easy to find that special home. But before you embarked on a breeding program, you knew you would come face to face with this reality. Having taken on the responsibility of bringing pups into the world, you now have the even more important responsibility of making sure they go to the best possible homes.

Advertising your litter in the newspapers is a good way to start. You can also announce your new arrivals in *Newf Tide*, the quarterly magazine published by The Newfoundland Club of America. (For the address, see page 94.) Many breeders will keep lists of families who are waiting for Newf puppies, so use your breeder-friend network to place your pups. Always screen prospective owners, alerting them to the pluses and minuses of owning a Newf. Be sure a prospective owner has a proper living arrangement to accommodate a giant breed like the Newf. As you have learned, Newfoundlands are not for everyone. But with perseverance and patience, you will make the perfect match between dog and owner. If you can't assure that, you shouldn't breed your Newf.

Proper Health Care for Your Newfoundland

Keeping Your Newf Healthy

Once you have brought your Newf home and integrated it into your family life, you have assumed a responsibility that goes far beyond just feeding and housing it. You must also make sure that it has a safe and healthy environment in which to grow and thrive. Remember, it's easier and far less costly, both monetarily and emotionally, to prevent common injuries and health problems before they arise. Earlier you learned that simple preventive care can save headaches and heartaches. You also need to learn how to protect your pet from the common diseases, parasites, and medical problems that will confront it during its life. Proper medical care is the best way to insure that your Newf will lead a happy, healthy, and long life.

As a dog owner, it's helpful to have a support system. Friends with dogs and breeders will be an invaluable part of that system. But by far, one of the most important relationships you and your Newf will establish is with your veterinarian. Availing yourself of his or her knowledge and skill will assure you that you are doing the very best for your Newf.

Once your Newf has had a week to acclimate to its new environment, schedule an appointment with your local veterinarian. If you don't have one, ask your doggy friends for their recommendations. Don't hesitate to interview prospective veterinarians before deciding on the one with which you and your Newf will feel most com-

fortable. You'll find most veterinarians are happy to answer any of your questions. They are as anxious as you to give your pet the best care possible. If he or she has experience with giant breeds like the Newf, all the better.

When you bring your Newf in for its first visit, your veterinarian will be able to properly evaluate its overall health. It's also important to get your Newf used to visiting the veterinarian's office during an unstressful time. That way, it will associate going there with pleasant things. When your Newf is full grown, you'll appreciate having a calm, well-behaved dog at the veterinarian's office instead of a giant dog that is unmanageable, frightened, and uncooperative.

Diseases Controlled by Immunizations

Throughout your Newf's life, you will have to make sure that it is vaccinated against some common canine diseases like distemper, rabies, parainfluenza, leptospirosis, hepatitis, coronavirus, and parvovirus. Immunization for these and other diseases is usually given in a series, beginning in early puppyhood. Your Newf should have received its first shots at the breeder's kennel when it was approximately six weeks old. Your veterinarian will then schedule follow-up vaccinations usually at the eight- to ten-week mark and then again at twelve weeks. The veterinarian will also immunize your Newf against bordatella (kennel cough). After completing its puppy series, your Newf will

To keep your Newf healthy and well-conditioned have it checked at least once a year for worms and other common parasites.

have to be revaccinated every year. It will also receive a rabies shot when it is between four to six months of age and, depending on the laws of the state in which you live, it'll need to be revaccinated every one to two years, according to local ordinances.

Distemper

Distemper is a viral disease that in its early stages most closely resembles a cold. Its symptoms include a runny nose, fever, loss of appetite, and listlessness, often accompanied by diarrhea. Occasionally, it causes the pads of the feet to thicken. As in any virus, its symptoms appear rapidly, within a week after exposure to an infected animal. Even if an affected dog appears to recover, the virus lingers, later manifesting itself in the form of convulsions, paralysis, twitching, and eventually, death. Because of the pernicious nature of the disease, it was one of the chief killers of puppies. However, with advances in modern medicine, and now that more and more animals are receiving vaccinations, the disease is nowhere near as common as it once was.

Rabies

Rabies is probably one of the most feared diseases known to afflict dogs and other mammals. It is an infectious disease that destroys the nerve cells of part of the brain and causes death. In Latin, the word means *rage* or *fury* and probably got that name because infected animals appeared mad and aggressive. However, contrary to popular belief, rabid dogs do not foam at the mouth. One of the symptoms of rabies is the inability to swallow water, resulting in saliva stringing from the mouth, due to paralysis of the jaw.

Rabies is not exclusively a canine disease, but affects all warm-blooded mammals, including humans. The most common carriers are wild ani-

mals like skunks, raccoons, foxes, and bats. It is transmitted by a bite from an infected animal and is always fatal. Thanks to a vaccine first developed in 1885 by Louis Pasteur, the disease is under control in domestic animals in most developed countries and has been virtually eradicated in England because of a mandate for quarantine. But it still exists in many parts of the world. Occasionally, there will be outbreaks in parts of the United States among the wild animal population. The disease is endemic in various regions of the United States in wild carnivores. Since the Newf is an active, outdoor dog, it is liable to come in contact with other animals. If it is not immunized against rabies and is bitten by a rabid animal, the consequences for it and even for you will be irreparable.

Infectious Canine Hepatitis

Infectious canine hepatitis, which is also a viral infection, can range from mild to severe. In its most virulent form, a sick dog can die within 24 hours of the first appearance of symptoms, which include: fever, listlessness, vomiting, abdominal tenderness and pain, tonsillitis, and hemorrhaging. Contact your veterinarian immediately if these symptoms appear.

Leptospirosis

Unlike distemper and hepatitis, leptospirosis is a spirochete disease. It is transmitted from dog to dog by exposure to an affected animal or by drinking water that has been contaminated with the urine of an infected animal. It can also be transmitted to many other mammals, including humans. Early signs of the disease include: loss of appetite, vomiting, diarrhea, and fever. Other signs are jaundice, abdominal pain, sores in the oral cavity, and weakness in the hindquarters. Once the disease has been allowed to advance untreated, kidney and liver damage can occur. Consult your veterinarian immediately if your dog has these symptoms.

Parvovirus

This viral disease is most deadly in puppies. Its symptoms mimic many other canine diseases and include: diarrhea, which is sometimes bloody, fever, and vomiting. Because dehydration occurs so quickly, your Newf's survival will depend on how quickly a diagnosis is made and treatment begun. With parvo, as with many canine diseases, the best treatment is prevention. By having your Newf vaccinated, you save it from becoming a victim of this terribly contagious disease.

Coronavirus

This highly contagious disease is every bit as devastating as parvovirus and very similar in symptomatology. Though coronavirus can be deadly to puppies, it can affect dogs of any age. Most puppy vaccines now contain protection against this virus; however, if your Newf has not been vaccinated and begins to exhibit symptoms that include an insidious and often foul-smelling, watery diarrhea that can be tinged with blood, isolate it and then take it to your veterinarian immediately.

Parainfluenza

Another highly contagious viral disease, parainfluenza can spread rapidly from one dog to another. It has often been erroneously termed "kennel cough" because of the dry hacking cough that develops. In fact, it causes an infectious tracheobronchitis characterized by a cough and retching to expel mucus. While it is not a fatal disease, parainfluenza can become debilitating and lowers the dog's resistance to secondary infections that can cause more serious medical problems. If your Newf

becomes infected, your veterinarian will have to treat it and isolate it from other dogs to keep the disease from spreading. As with other contagious canine diseases, the best cure is vaccination before the fact.

Bordetella

Bordetella is a bacterial infection that is often put under the generalized term "kennel cough." Its symptoms include a hacking cough, runny nose, and weepy eyes. In fact, it is often seen in conjunction with tracheobronchitis. To immunize your Newf, the veterinarian will squirt the vaccine into the dog's nostrils rather than inject it. While your pet probably won't like the sensation, the protection it will get is worth the momentary discomfort. Some dogs have been known to come down with mild symptoms within 10 days after vaccination. If this happens, don't worry. Your pet isn't contagious—it will just look and sound like it is!

Lyme Disease

Since the Newf loves the outdoors, it is very likely that you and your pet will spend time romping in parks, woods, or around lakes. Unfortunately, these are all breeding grounds for the minuscule deer tick that can carry Lyme disease. First identified in the town of Lyme, Connecticut, Lyme disease is a serious malady that can affect both you and your Newf. It is transmitted by a bite from a carrier tick. In dogs, the disease is usually characterized by tenderness and swelling in the joints. In humans, the symptoms are not always so recognizable and can mimic other illnesses, particularly flu. If you suspect you have been bitten by a tick and notice a small, circular rash developing at the site of the bite, see your physician or call a Lyme disease hotline immediately. While there is no vaccine available for humans at present, there is one for your pet. Your veterinarian will administer the Lyme vaccination in an initial series of two injections, spaced over a three-week period. Thereafter, your Newf will need a yearly booster.

Parasites

The blight of parasites poses one of the greatest annoyances to both pets and their owners. A parasite is an animal that lives in or on an organism of another species that acts as its host. External parasites like fleas and ticks, as well as internal ones like worms, can make your Newf's life and yours miserable. Fortunately, you can get a handle on the situation by following a regimen that begins with keeping your pet's quarters clean. No matter how conscientious you are, however, the reality is that at some time during your Newf's life, it will be infected with parasites. Knowing what to look for and understanding how to eliminate the problem is half the battle.

External Parasites

Fleas. The word alone sends chills up many a dog owner's spine! It's easy to understand why, since this pest causes more skin and coat problems among dogs than any other parasite. Just consider this: there are 11,000 different types of fleas! In cases of severe infestation, the flea, which feeds on the dog's blood supply, can cause your Newf to develop anemia. Your Newf can also contract tapeworm by ingesting a single flea. Some dogs also develop an allergic reaction to fleas. For this reason, you should consult your veterinarian and decide on a course of prevention and treatment before the problem gets out of hand. Once the flea gets in the house and into carpets, cracks, or crevices, it's total war!

The lifecycle of the flea explains why. A single female flea can lay hundreds of eggs that hatch and become adults in under three weeks. As the mating process continues and multiplies, it won't take long for your home to become infested. In order to combat the problem, you must launch an attack on every front. Flea dips, shampoos, and powders, as well as flea collars can kill fleas on your dog. However, you must also treat your house and the rest of the dog's environment at the same time or your efforts will be useless. Flea foggers can be used in the house, but for cases of severe infestation, particularly in warmer climates, a professional exterminator may be needed. There are also other flea control products on the market, including a nontoxic borax-based powder that breaks the lifecycle of the flea by preventing it from reproducing. The product, sold under a variety of generic names, is brushed into the carpet once a year and is highly effective. Flea pills are also available from your veterinarian, as well as a new series of flea shots. However, before using any flea product, consult your veterinarian who will advise you on the best method of prevention.

Ticks. Since your Newf loves the outdoors and particularly enjoys a romp in the woods, it may pick up ticks. There are many types of ticks, including the deer tick that carries Lyme disease, as discussed on page 79. But by far the most common is the brown dog tick. These insidious parasites are found in woods and fields where they cling to vegetation and then attach themselves to animals. If you live in a wooded area, make sure to check your Newf after walks or exercise periods by running your hands up and down its extremities and around its neck and ears, which are the most common places for ticks to congregate. If you find a tick burrowed in, you can remove it yourself by dabbing it with alcohol or nail polish remover. This may cause the tick to loosen its hold momentarily. Then take a tweezers and grab it as close to the skin as possible and pull it

When you purchase your Newfoundland pup, be sure it has been checked for subvalvular aortic stenosis (SAS), which can affect the pup by nine weeks of age.

out. Be careful to disengage it completely and not leave any of the mouthpiece in the dog's skin because infection can result. Dispose of the tick and then treat the bite with a dab of alcohol or antibiotic cream.

Ear Mites. If you notice your Newf scratching or rubbing its ears with its pause, or shaking its head, ear mites could be the problem. Check the ears and, if you see dark, waxy, foul-smelling matter, take the dog to the veterinarian so a definitive diagnosis can be made. Mites are microscopic bugs that live in your dog's ear canal. By examining the residue in the dog's ear, your veterinarian will easily be able to identify the problem. If your Newf does have mites, your veterinarian will clean out the ears and give you medication to correct the problem. Since mites can be transmitted from one animal to another, if you have other pets in the house, including cats, you must have them checked as well.

Mange. At one time, the word "mange" was enough to make many a dog owner shutter. This skin disorder, characterized by scaly, oozing patches, is caused by another type of mite that burrows into the epidermis and causes the dog to scratch, bite, and lose its hair. There are several types of mange, but the most common are: red mange, also called demodectic, and scabies, also called sarcoptic.

While all dogs carry mites in the pores of their skin, they almost never become "active" and cause problems unless the dog is under stress. Red mange is seen more frequently in puppies and older dogs. In its early stages, it is easily treatable and may even disappear by itself. Scabies, on the other hand, requires immediate treatment and is contagious.

81

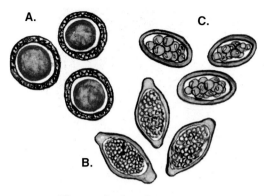

Microscopic view of worms:
A: Roundworm eggs;
B: Whipworm eggs;
C: Hookworm eggs.

Regardless of the type of mange you suspect, consult your veterinarian so the problem can be correctly identified and treated, if necessary.

Internal Parasites

During the course of its life, your Newf will probably have worms. The four most common types are: roundworms, hookworms, whipworms, and tapeworms. The first three can easily be diagnosed by your veterinarian by examination of a fecal specimen under a microscope.

Tapeworms are transmitted when a dog swallows an infected flea or rodent and can be seen by the naked eye in the dog's stool or attached to hair around the anal area. Tapeworm segments detach from the worm. They are pale pink in color and resemble flattened grains of rice. If untreated, tapeworms can cause your dog to lose weight and become generally debilitated.

Roundworms are found more commonly in puppies than in older dogs. Puppies can be born with this parasite if the mother is infected. They are passed on to other dogs through the excreted feces where the eggs are present. Suspect roundworms if your Newf's coat becomes dull or its abdomen seems to hang like a pot belly. It may also expel the worms in vomit or in stool. They resemble long, whitish, spaghetti-like strands.

Whipworms are found in the large intestine. Symptoms include diarrhea, loss of weight, restlessness, and anemia if the infestation goes untreated. Keeping your Newf's kennel clean is imperative to prevent it from contracting this parasite. However, while whipworms and others are contagious, they don't self-generate because of a dirty kennel; they are passed from dog to dog.

Hookworms can affect dogs of any age, but they affect puppies more dramatically. They attach themselves inside the small intestine and suck blood from the intestinal wall. A puppy with hookworms will lose appetite and weight and will often have bloody or black stools. If untreated, anemia can result and in puppies this can be fatal.

Heartworms are transmitted to your dog by a mosquito bite. The carrier mosquito deposits microfilariae that are then transported through the dog's bloodstream, finally lodging in the heart where they mature and reproduce. When the carrier dog is bitten by an uninfected mosquito, the mosquito then becomes infected and bites another dog and the vicious cycle continues. If not diagnosed and treated, heart failure will be the end result. However, diagnosis is difficult and treatment is risky so the safest path is prevention. Before your veterinarian puts your Newf on a program, it must first be given a simple blood test to be sure no heartworms are present. Once that is determined, your Newf will be put on a heartworm preventative medication. Three different types are currently available: a tablet (Filaribits), given once daily during mosquito season; a liquid (Caricide), added to the food daily; or a tablet (Heartguard) given monthly. Most dogs should remain on a preventative throughout the mosquito season (spring, summer, fall). But if you live in a warm, moist climate, you should keep your Newf on preventative all year round. Every year, your veterinarian will give your Newf an occult blood test to make sure it is heartworm free.

Coccidia and Giardia are commonly found in puppies. Both are more difficult to identify than most common worms. Diagnosis requires a careful examination of a fresh fecal sample by your veterinarian. Signs to watch for that may signal the presence of these protozoas are weight loss, watery diarrhea, and dullness of coat.

A wise rule of thumb is to have your Newf routinely checked for the presence of worms during its yearly visit to the veterinarian's office.

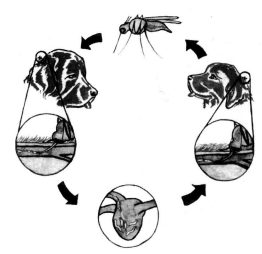

The lifecycle of the heartworm. Your Newf can contract heartworm after being bitten by an infected mosquito.

Common Illnesses and Medical Problems

No matter how diligent a "parent" you are, at one time or another during its life, your Newfy "child" will encounter common medical problems—so don't panic. Fortunately, most illnesses can be treated and you and your Newf can get back to the business of living, loving, and playing together.

Constipation, Diarrhea, and Vomiting

Occasionally, your Newf may experience a change in its bowel movements. This can be brought on by something as simple as changing its diet or stress. If the dog suddenly appears to be straining, suspect constipation. This is usually a nonemergency problem that will correct itself. If it persists, or if the dog appears to be in pain when it tries to defecate, call your veterinarian at once.

Like constipation, diarrhea and vomiting can be triggered by a change in diet or stress. Worms can also be the culprit. If either diarrhea or vomiting becomes severe and lasts more than 12 hours, suspect a more serious condition and call your veterinarian. Both conditions can lead to extreme dehydration that is often fatal in young puppies. Until you are thoroughly familiar with what is normal for your Newf, don't hesitate to call the veterinarian at the first sign of a change in its daily behavior.

Impacted Anal Sacs

If your Newf starts "scooting" its rear end on the ground, suspect impacted anal sacs. These two glands lie on either side of the rectum, just inside the anus. Occasionally, they can become clogged or impacted. When that happens, they must be emptied out manually to avoid more serious conditions like infection or abscess. The first time it happens, take your dog to the veterinarian and let him or her show you what to do if the problem

After eating, your Newf should avoid strenuous activity for 1–2 hours to decrease its chances of bloating.

Unfortunately, bloat is being seen more and more among dogs of all breeds; however, it is believed that large, deep-chested dogs like the Newfoundland are at a much greater risk. There is no way to predict whether a dog will bloat at some time during its life. At best, you can only exercise preventative measures based on current information available and learn to recognize the danger signs because, if your Newf does bloat, your quick action can save its life.

Though research continues about the causes of bloat, there is still no clear-cut answer. Current data seems to suggest there may be a link between food and bloat. The condition is triggered when the stomach swells up from gas, fluid, or a combination of the two. Once the stomach becomes distended, it has a tendency to twist. Be on the lookout for the following signs:
• swollen stomach and abdominal pain
• excessive drooling
• unsuccessful attempts to vomit or defecate
• inability to find a comfortable position
• cool, pale skin and gums

If you suspect bloat, don't waste a second, get your Newf to the veterinarian IMMEDIATELY. It's far better to be wrong about its condition than to risk losing it to this horrible and painful killer.

As a preventative measure, it's wise to divide your Newf's daily food allotment into at least two separate meals per day. Don't exercise it an hour before or after eating and limit its intake of water after exercise.

arises again. To empty the anal sacs, you must apply pressure to both sides of each gland. A thick, odoriferous secretion will then be expelled. Repeat the same procedure with the other sac. It may not be the most pleasant job in the house, but as the saying goes, somebody's got to do it!

Gastric Torsion or Bloat

A serious and often fatal problem is gastric torsion, also known as bloat. In fact, they are two separate conditions. A dog whose stomach bloats often "twists" as well, thus the term "gastric torsion."

Tumors

Like the human population, the dog world is also plagued with another potential killer, cancer. However, it is important to realize that not every growth, lump, or bump you may find on your dog is cancer. In fact, most are benign growths or

84

cysts. As a breed, Newfoundlands are prone to all kinds of lumps and bumps, both internally and externally, but fortunately, most are noncancerous. Just to be sure, any time you notice a lump or swelling on any part of its body, let your veterinarian check it out. You should get into the habit of manually going over your Newf's body once a week. Make it a regular part of its grooming. That way, you will know its body and be alerted to any irregularities.

If your Newf should develop cancer during its lifetime, don't lose heart. As with humans, cancer isn't necessarily a death sentence. Depending on the type of tumor your dog has, your veterinarian can advise you of the types of treatment available.

Common Health Problems in Newfoundlands

Hip Dysplasia

Since the Newfoundland is considered a giant breed, it is particularly prone to orthopedic problems. One of the more prevalent is hip dysplasia, which can take many forms. The most common form is a condition in which the ball of the hip joint doesn't fit securely into the socket. The resulting friction causes the ball and socket to wear down in some places and build up abnormally in others. To make matters worse, arthritis often sets in as well, and the pet becomes increasingly uncomfortable as the condition deteriorates. While many dysplastic dogs can live long, productive lives with very little distress, others will require anti-inflammatory painkillers. In some cases, the dysplasia is so crippling that the dog may have to be euthanized. Surgery is another option, but is not successful in every case.

The best way to avoid dysplasia is to choose your Newf puppy carefully. Since research has shown that dysplasia is primarily genetic, study your

One of the orthopedic problems that can affect giant breeds like the Newf is hip dysplasia. An X-ray can determine whether or not your pet is dysplastic.

prospective pup's ancestry. If its parents and grandparents are nondysplastic, there's a fairly good chance it will be, too. The only way to be sure your Newf is not dysplastic is to have its hips X rayed after it reaches two years of age. Your veterinarian can evaluate the films but you can also have them checked by an independent agency called the Orthopedic Foundation for Animals (OFA), which is composed of expert veterinary radiologists who examine the dog's hip X rays and then determine if they are within the normal range for the breed. If the OFA determines that your dog is nondysplastic, it will assign it an OFA number. Before buying your Newf, it is wise to be certain both its parents have OFA numbers. An alternative to the OFA X rays is a new method developed at the University of Pennsylvania called PENNHIP. With this method, a dog can be X rayed as young as six months old and the owner can be given a fairly accurate description of the hips. If you are buying a dog for show, or breeding dogs, PENNHIP may be the best way to be assured your Newf does not have hip dysplasia.

You can also take precautions to insure that your Newf doesn't develop other orthopedic problems by not allowing it to put on extra weight at any age. Be especially mindful of extra pounds while it's still a pup and its bones are forming. If your Newf is dysplastic, obesity will only compound the problem.

Heart Disease

Another serious problem that can affect the Newfoundland breed is heart disease, particularly subvalvular aortic stenosis (SAS). This disease is also prevalent in other breeds. Like hip dysplasia, studies have found that SAS is inherited, but even a Newf that's declared clear of the disease can still produce it in the progeny. The reason is unclear. We do know that SAS is not present at birth, but develops as the puppy grows. This is another reason you should have your Newf checked by your veterinarian early, preferably after nine weeks of age. If SAS is present, it is detectable as a murmur ranging from slight to severe. Responsible breeders will have their litters evaluated by a veterinary cardiologist before the pups leave their kennel for their new homes. Unfortunately, there are no guarantees with SAS. Newfoundlands diagnosed with a mild form of the disease can live long, productive lives or they can die at an early age.

Even though many murmurs in Newfs turn out to be SAS, many others are functional murmurs, which are temporary and not harmful to the dog. A functional murmur can sound like SAS, but unlike SAS, it will disappear within a few weeks to a few months. Only your veterinarian can make the proper diagnosis.

Eye Problems

Entropion, or the turning in of the eyelid, is another genetic problem sometimes found in the Newfoundland breed. As the lid turns in, it allows the eyelashes to rub against the cornea, which causes inflammation, irritation, and pain. Surgery is necessary to correct the condition.

Ectropion is a problem in which the opposite occurs: the eyelid turns outward, sagging and exposing the eye to irritants like dirt and dust and other pollutants. Most ectropic dogs can function very well without corrective surgery.

All dogs have three eyelids: an upper, a lower, and a third inner eyelid that is usually out of sight. Sometimes the third eyelid can prolapse or pop out and a mass of red tissue will be seen at the inside corner of the eye. This condition, aptly named "cherry eye," is usually seen more in young dogs. Initially it affects only one eye, but the other eye often becomes infected within a few weeks. Cherry eye can be caused by a trauma, but it is also a common congenital defect that can be passed on from one generation to another. The condition can be permanently corrected by surgically removing the gland of the third eyelid.

Emergency Care

One of the most important things to learn is what to do if a medical emergency should arise. The first rule: Don't panic; then seek immediate advice from your veterinarian.

Poisoning

In our efforts to protect our canine friends from parasites, we have unfortunately introduced more and more toxic substances into the household. Products like flea dips, flea collars, sprays, and disinfectants can cause skin irritations and sometimes a dangerously toxic condition. For this reason, it's best to check with your veterinarian before using a pesticide in your home or on your lawn.

There are also other household products that can be lethal to your pet if ingested. One of the most common culprits is antifreeze, which is routinely stored in garages. The liquid is sweet-tasting and appealing to dogs; it is dangerously poisonous. Soap, detergents, and boric acid can also be lethal, as well as paint, fertilizer, and other garden supplies. For safety's sake, it's wise to pet-proof all of your kitchen cabinets and keep your garage or tool shed locked at all times. Under no circumstances should you leave your Newf unattended in a garage where many of these items are likely to be stored.

Since your Newf will be outdoors a lot, it could also pick something up without your knowing it. Be alert to signs of poisoning that include: vomiting, labored breathing, stomach cramps, trembling, disorientation, and a change in the color of the mucous membranes. If you suspect poisoning, call your veterinarian immediately.

Accidents

Every year, road accidents claim an enormous number of animal lives. Most of these can be prevented if pet owners exercised more diligence. When you walk your Newf, always keep it on a lead. No matter how well trained you believe it is, a stimulus like a rabbit or a squirrel scurrying by can send it across a street and into the path of a moving vehicle with fatal results. Never open the door and allow it to take itself for a walk. If you have a fenced yard, make sure gates are always latched before you let your dog out.

Of course, accidents happen with even the most alert owners. If your Newf is injured in an accident of any kind, get it to the veterinarian immediately—but first exercise some simple precautions. Remember, an injured animal is a frightened animal. To avoid being bitten, secure a makeshift muzzle around its jaws. Use a belt, a tie, whatever is available, and gently wrap it around its mouth. Move it very carefully if internal injuries are suspected and take it right to the veterinarian.

Bleeding

If your Newf is hurt or is bleeding, determine the point of the bleeding and then apply firm, direct pressure to the spot. If the cut or wound is deep, your Newf will probably require sutures. If there is profuse bleeding from any extremity, you can apply a tourniquet. To make a tourniquet, wrap a cloth or belt or whatever else is handy, between the injury and the heart. Then loosen it for 15 to 30 seconds every 15 minutes. Be aware that tourniquets can be dangerous if you don't know what you're doing. If in doubt, apply direct pressure to the wound. Anything but minor bleeding should be treated as a medical emergency and your Newf should be taken to the veterinarian immediately.

Heatstroke

You and your Newf will undoubtedly get used to traveling together, but be forewarned that the car can be a potential death trap for a dog in hot weather in less than ten minutes. Don't be fooled by the weather outside. It doesn't have to be 90°F (32°C) for your dog to succumb to heatstroke inside the car. Even if you leave the windows

You may need to administer CPR if your Newf has been in an accident.

into the mouth. Make sure the chest is expanding with every breath. Repeat every five to six seconds until it is breathing on its own, then get it to the veterinarian. If your dog has a head, neck, or spinal injury, however, using the above method can cause a violent reaction. Also be aware that reaching into the mouth of an injured animal that is conscious can pose a danger to you in the form of a bite.

Proper Dental Care

No discussion about how to care for your Newf's health would be complete without mentioning dental hygiene. Remember, your Newf's teeth and gums need just as much attention as the rest of its body does. A dental exam should be a part of its yearly medical checkup. Fortunately, dogs' teeth are usually in better condition than human teeth because they don't usually snack on candy bars and other sweets. However, dogs do build up calculus and tartar on their teeth and, if left untreated, periodontal problems can result. Chew toys and nylon bones will help keep your Newf's teeth clean, but only daily brushing will prevent tartar build-up.

If you get your Newf used to having its teeth brushed from puppyhood, it will soon regard it as a pleasant part of its daily grooming ritual. Your veterinarian will instruct you on the proper method of brushing your dog's teeth and give you a special brush and

open several inches, in direct sunlight on a pleasant 60°F (15.6°C) day, the car can heat up enough to kill your beloved pet. You should also never leave your Newf outside in hot weather without some form of shelter from the sun. Be alert to the signs of heatstroke, which include: rapid panting, bright red gums, a dazed look, and high fever. If you observe any of these symptoms, take immediate action. Place cool, moist compresses or towels all over its body, accompanied by an ice pack to get the temperature down. Then rush it to the veterinarian.

CPR

If your Newf is injured in an accident, it may require artificial respiration. Administer CPR by first opening its mouth and checking for any obstructions. Then pull out its tongue to make sure nothing is caught in the pharynx. Next, clear the mouth of any mucus or blood. Keep the mouth slightly open and with one hand, hold the tongue firmly to the bottom of the mouth and, with the other hand, cover the nostrils. Then begin blowing air

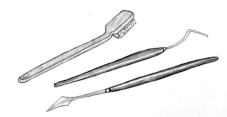

Proper dental care is essential to your Newf's good health. Your veterinarian can demonstrate the correct use of dental tools.

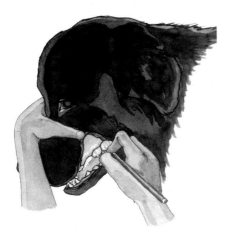

A tooth scaler will help you to remove plaque and calculus that accumulates on your Newf's teeth.

toothpaste to use. Do not attempt to use human toothpaste as it can be harmful to your pet. There are also several anti-plaque gels on the market that you can rub into your Newf's gums on a regular basis. This will keep plaque and calculus from building up and save you the expense of professional cleanings. You can also purchase a professional tooth scaler from wholesale dog catalogs. Your veterinarian or veterinary technician can demonstrate the proper way to scale your dog's teeth between visits.

Also keep in mind that puppies love to chew just about anything, so be sure to supervise what goes into its mouth. Don't allow it to chew hard objects like rocks because a broken or chipped tooth is likely to result.

Once again, common sense and prevention are the keys. If you keep your Newf's teeth and gums healthy, it won't be plagued by decaying teeth that can cause other health problems as it gets older.

Administering Medicine

At different times during your Newf's life, you will invariably have to admin-ister medication. If you need to give it liquid medicine, it's more easily accomplished with the aid of a small syringe, which you can fill with the prescribed amount of medication. Then pull the lips away from the side of your Newf's mouth, insert the syringe, and dispense the medicine. To administer tablets, open your Newf's mouth, hold its head slightly back, and place the pill as far to the rear of the tongue as possible. Then hold its mouth closed with one hand and stroke its neck with the other to activate the swallowing impulse. Be sure not to hold its head too far back because the pill could become lodged in the windpipe rather than down the throat. Often, giving the dog a bit of cheese or other treat immediately afterward will assure that the pill has been swallowed. Most important, make sure it doesn't spit it out!

One of the hardest things for any dog owner to do is to make the decision to have a beloved pet "put to sleep," when, either through disease or old age, it can no longer enjoy a good quality of life.

Caring for the Older Newfoundland

When your Newf reaches the age of seven, by dog standards it will be well into middle age. As it ages, it will become less active and its nutritional needs will change (see page 51). Generally, it will need a diet with less, though higher quality protein. But make no mistake, your Newf is still capable of being a vital member of the family and, if you've cared for it well during its younger years, there is no reason why it shouldn't live to a ripe old age, which for a Newfoundland is around 12 years. However, you should be aware of physical changes that occur as your dog gets older. Pay particular attention to its teeth and gums and any changes in its bladder or bowel habits. Its eyesight and hearing may also become impaired as it ages. Dogs, like humans, are also afflicted with arthritis and rheumatism, but these conditions are often managed with little difficulty. Since your Newf has been your faithful friend and companion for so many years, you will be happy to make its advanced years as enjoyable and comfortable as possible. Remember, the worst disease that can afflict your Newf as it ages is neglect. Good preventative care throughout its lifetime is the best way to assure it of a long and healthy life.

Euthanasia

It has been called the ultimate kindness. Nonetheless, when and if the time comes to put your Newf down, it will be one of the saddest moments in your life. If your dog, either because of advanced age or terminal illness, has reached a point where it is in pain or can no longer enjoy a good quality of life, putting it to sleep is probably the kindest thing you can do for your most loyal and loving companion. Most Newfs, unless stricken by fatal illness or accident, will live long, healthy lives. As the years go by, you will watch it go from a young ball of fire to a robust adult to a more mellow senior citizen. Finally, at some point, you will realize that every day is a struggle for it. Whether it becomes a victim of illness or advanced old age, your Newf will no longer be capable of dealing with even the most basic of daily routines. Making the decision to say good-bye is the hardest, as well as the most unselfish one, you will ever have to face. Don't try to make it alone. Seek the support of the whole family and, most importantly, seek the advice of your veterinarian, who has known you and your Newf over the years. Often, there are options besides euthanasia and your veterinarian can best advise you if treating your pet is possible or realistic. Whatever your decision, be comforted that you have made it totally and completely out of love for the best friend you have had or will ever have, your beloved Newfy.

Famous Newfoundlands and Their Owners

As you have already read in these pages, Newfoundlands have found their way into history and the limelight on occasions too numerous to mention. The breed's gentle nature combined with the loyal and loving qualities that make Newfs excellent companions and working dogs have earned them a deservedly special place in the hearts of enthusiasts everywhere. Perhaps that's why Newf owners delight in trading their stories and exchanging legends of Newfs past and present.

During the American colonial period, two famous Newfs belonged to our first president, George Washington and to statesman, Benjamin Franklin. Another celebrated Newf, Samuel Adams' dog, QueQue, used to make it a point to annoy the British troops in Boston (see Origins and History of the Breed on page 8). England's Queen Victoria was also a great Newf enthusiast.

Americans are probably most familiar with a huge black Newf named Brumis who was the devoted companion of the late Robert F. Kennedy. It's said that while Kennedy served as United States Attorney General, Brumis could be seen scampering through the halls of the Justice Department. It's further reported that the big Newf "sat in" by its master's feet during many top secret, strategic meetings. Perhaps that's why Brumis would steal away, unobserved, to the FBI section of the building from time to time! Political satirist Art Buchwald once wrote that any dinner guest at the Kennedy house had better hold onto his or her plate because, given the slightest opportunity, Brumis would jump up and make a clean sweep of everything on the table! Obviously the Kennedys were undaunted. They later acquired three more Newfs.

The late crooner Bing Crosby was also a Newf fan. He began breeding them in the 1940s and gave a puppy from one of his litters to President Franklin D. Roosevelt as a special gift for the children of the Warm Springs Foundation. Boomer Esiason, quarterback for the New York Jets, is another famous Newf fancier. Two of his dogs were bred by his family's Ebonewf Kennels.

Many Newfoundlands have found their own way to fame and celebrity in the movies. Theatergoers are perhaps most familiar with a great bronze-colored Newf named Kodiak who played the dog named Lou in the hit comedy, *Police Academy 2*. The dog also has the honor of being the most titled Newf in the history of the breed, but you could say Kodiak's stardom went to his head. According to reports, after his initial brush with fame the dog began to ignore directors and would actually walk off the set if he thought a scene had been shot too many times! However, along with his apparently big ego, Kodiak had a big heart as well. The Newf was a real

Throughout the ages, Newfoundlands have been the preferred canine companions of many famous people.

life hero when he saved his owner from perishing after her house filled with smoke when she drifted off to sleep with the stove on.

The Newfoundland has also made its way to fame in literature. *The Animal Book*, which is a collection of short tales compiled by W. H. Kingston, contains several accounts of Newfoundlands. Author Marie Killilea wrote a very special children's book titled *Newf*, which is a beautifully written and illustrated account of a big black dog that appears on a remote coastline and befriends a small white kitten. It is a tale of love,

devotion, and bravery and is a must-read for fanciers, children, and adults alike. Another book, an anthology entitled, *Brave Tales of Real Dogs* by Eleanor Fairchild Pease, recounts the tale of a Scottish Newf who rescued a mastiff, which happened to be its arch enemy, from drowning. The book also describes feats of daring and bravery by other Newfs.

With a history and following as rich and loyal as this great breed enjoys, you'll be glad you chose the Newfoundland to be your loving friend and companion for the rest of its life.

The Newfoundland has also been immortalized in art, literature, and most recently, in films.

Useful Literature and Addresses

International Kennel Clubs

The Newfoundland Club of
America
Mrs. Robert M. Price
Membership Secretary
4908 Rolling Green Parkway
Edina, MN 55436

The American Kennel Club
51 Madison Avenue
New York, NY 10038

The Canadian Kennel Club
100-89 Skyway Avenue
Etobicoke, Ontario
Canada M9W 6R4

Information and Publications

Newf Tide—magazine of The
Newfoundland Club of
America
Linda McCormick, editor
195 Dollywood Drive
P.O. Box 160
Toney, AL 35773

AKC Tracking Regulations
c/o The American Kennel
Club
51 Madison Avenue
New York, NY 10038

*Newfoundland Club of America
Water Test Rules and
Regulations and Training
Manual*
Att. Joyce Echon
P.O. Box 142
Stevens Point, WI 54481

*CKC Regulations and
Standards for Tracking Tests*
c/o The Canadian Kennel
Club
100-89 Skyway Avenue
Etobicoke, Ontario
Canada M9W 6R4

Associations

American Veterinary Medical
Association
930 North Meacham Rd.
Schaumburg, IL 60173

Orthopedic Foundation for
Animals (OFA)
2300 E. Nifong Blvd.
Columbia, MO 65201

Books

Adler, Judi. *The Newfoundland
Puppy: Early Care, Early
Training*. Third Edition,
(1993). From the author,
12320 SW Malloy, Sherwood,
Oregon 97140.

———. *The Audible Nose*.
From the author, 12320 SW
Malloy, Sherwood, Oregon
97140.

———. *Water Work, Water
Play*. From the author, 12320
SW Malloy, Sherwood,
Oregon 97140.

Bendure, Joan C. *The
Newfoundland, Companion
Dog—Water Dog*. Howell
House, Inc., New York, New
York: 1994.

Klever, Ulrich. *The Complete
Book of Dog Care*. Barron's
Educational Series, Inc.,
Hauppauge, New York: 1989.

Powell, Consie. *Newfoundland
Draft Work: A Guide for
Training*. From the author,
5208 Olive Rd., Raleigh,
North Carolina: 27606.

Ullmann, Hans. *The New Dog
Handbook*. Barron's
Educational Series, Inc.,
Hauppauge, New York: 1984.

Index